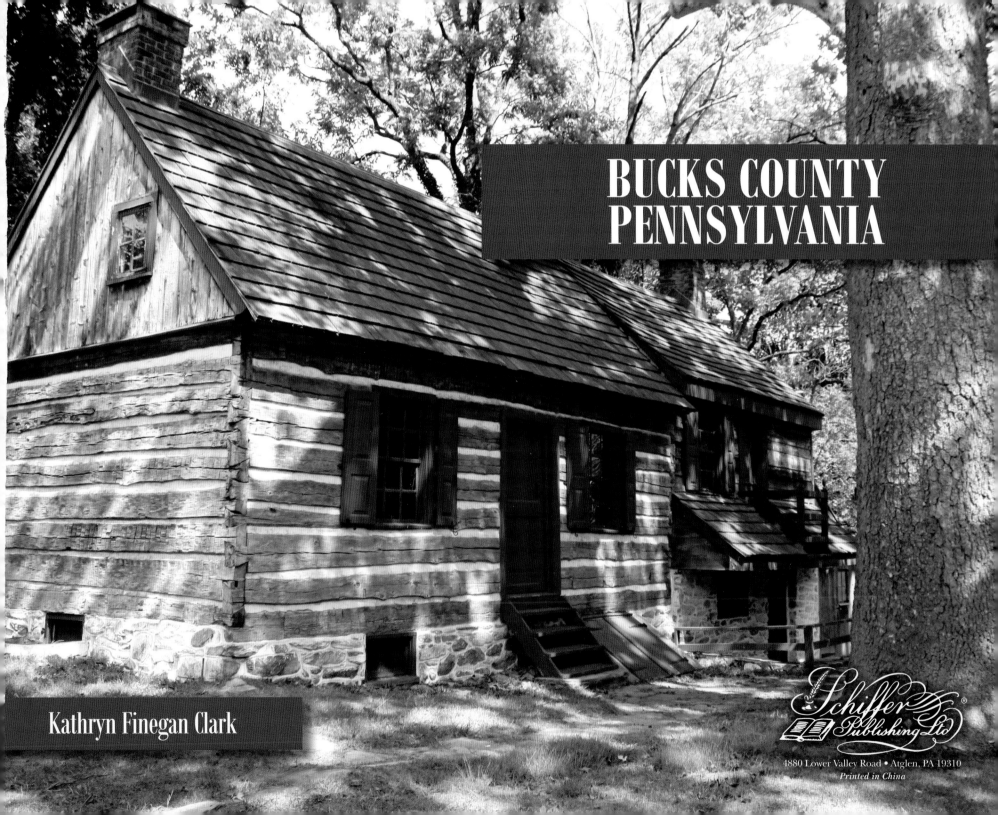

BUCKS COUNTY PENNSYLVANIA

Kathryn Finegan Clark

Schiffer Publishing Ltd

4880 Lower Valley Road • Atglen, PA 19310
Printed in China

Schiffer Books are available at special discounts for bulk purchases for sales promotions or premiums. Special editions, including personalized covers, corporate imprints, and excerpts can be created in large quantities for special needs. For more information contact the publisher:

Published by Schiffer Publishing Ltd.
4880 Lower Valley Road
Atglen, PA 19310
Phone: (610) 593-1777; Fax: (610) 593-2002
E-mail: Info@schifferbooks.com

For the largest selection of fine reference books on this and related subjects, please visit our website at:
www.schifferbooks.com
We are always looking for people to write books on new and related subjects. If you have an idea for a book,
please contact us at
proposals@schifferbooks.com

This book may be purchased from the publisher.
Please try your bookstore first.
You may write for a free catalog.

In Europe, Schiffer books are distributed by
Bushwood Books
6 Marksbury Ave.
Kew Gardens
Surrey TW9 4JF England
Phone: 44 (0) 20 8392 8585; Fax: 44 (0) 20 8392 9876
E-mail: info@bushwoodbooks.co.uk
Website: www.bushwoodbooks.co.uk

Dedication

For my husband, Jack, who has been with me every step of the way; and, for their loving encouragement and support, our daughter, Stephanie, and her husband, Dale; our son, Evan, and his wife, Jeanna, and our grandson, Emmett.

Acknowledgments

The author greatly appreciates the kindness of those who helped provide information for this book. Their names, in no particular order, follow:

Edward S. Henning, Agent for the Lenape Nation of Pennsylvania
Carol Kuhn, Docent at the Sigal Museum in Easton, Pennsylvania
Donna Carcaci Rhodes, Curator, Pearl S. Buck House
Mary Ellen Kunz of Pennsbury Manor
Joe Ferry of Perkasie Olde Town Association
Rosanne McCarty of Old St. John's Church
Margaret A. McKevitt of the Bucks County Planning Commission
Barry Cyphers, Head Gardener at Andalusia
Marge Custer, Director of Lenape Village, Churchville Nature Center
Edward L. Reidell, Site Administrator, Fonthill Museum
Heather Hicks, Education Assistant, Fonthill and Mercer Museums
Sally Van Sant Sondesky and **Victoria MacDougall** of the Bensalem Historical Society
Robert F. Hueston, Ph.D, Professor Emeritus of American History, University of Scranton.
Carolyn Calkins Smith of Calkins Media Incorporated
Linda Cooper, former clerk of Richland Friends Meeting
Susan and Curt Yeske, fellow journalists
Bridget Wingert of the Bucks County Herald
Joseph M. Kulick, Durham Township Manager
Edward Levenson, historian and editor, Doylestown Historical Society
Cory Amsler, Vice President, Collections and Interpretation, Mercer Museum
Janet and **Francis Lavenger**
Bradley Sullivan of Sullivan Building & Design Group
Candace Clarke of the James A. Michener Art Museum
Soomi Hahn Amagasu of George Nakashima Woodworker, S.A.
Myron and **LeeAnn Kressman**
Bert Nicholas
Mary Elizabeth Hartz
Brendan Hartz
Justin Hartz
Edward T. Finegan III
Karl Schwartz

CONTENTS

INTRODUCTION

Bucks County is carved into fifty-four municipalities, though only the townships are shown here. They often surround smaller boroughs that bear the same name, such as Bristol and Bristol Township.

A Study in Contrasts

*B*ucks County, if anything, is a study in contrasts.

It's the oldest of the old, newest of the new; almost-urban, suburban, and rural. It's the oldest town in the southern portion, oldest industry in the far north.

Flat coastal plain in the southern part, rolling hills in the central part, jagged cliffs, steep, rocky slopes, streams, rock-strewn pastures and meadows clustered in the Durham Hills in the north.

Six million tourists come here every year. Even in the 1600s, colonists traveled the fifty or so miles between Bristol, the county's earliest town, and the Durham iron mines in the far north. Their passage left behind a network of old inns along a wagon trail that now is Pennsylvania Route 611.

Bucks County lives comfortably with its past, but it's not entrenched there. It's a vital and exciting place, full of energy and plans for the future.

Tourists often find themselves in horse-drawn carriages riding side by side with farmers' plows and pickups, Mercedes, stretch limousines, tourist trolleys, and buses.

The third oldest of William Penn's original counties, Bucks County was founded in 1682. It not only retains a charm that has made it a tourist Mecca, but also is a superb place to live. Its strategic location between Philadelphia and New York has contributed to its place among the one hundred wealthiest counties in the

New Hope's sidewalks and stores offer a quirky charm for tourists in Central Bucks County.

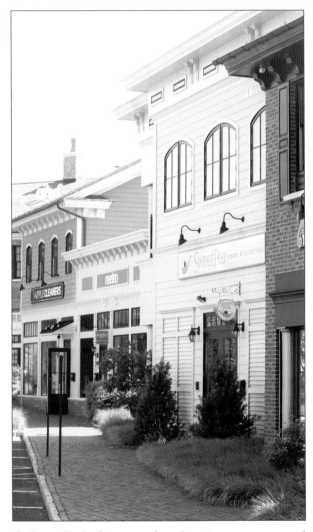

In Lower Bucks County, modern shopping centers surround historic places such as Newtown.

United States. In 2008, *LIFE* magazine named Bucks County one of its "Dream Destinations: The World's 100 Best Places to Vacation."

However, we should not forget that it was also a dream destination in the late 1600s when William Penn opened his new territory to people of all religions. He built his country home not far from the King's Highway connecting, at the time, Manhattan Island and the lower valley of the Delaware River, roughly paralleling what is now U.S. Route 1. Once an Indian path, it ran close to the river, traveled by the early Dutch, the Swedes, and the English.

It is not possible to live here without stumbling into history at every turn. At latest count, the National Register of Historic Places listed 155 properties in Bucks County; eight are also designated National Historic Landmarks.

Bucks County is big as counties go — about fifty miles from north to south and thirty miles at its widest from east to west. In many ways it remains a county divided, a place where sophistication lies side by side with provincialism. Farmers who rarely leave their fields live next to people who commute daily to New York City, Philadelphia or cities in New Jersey.

For years, the county has also been divided into three geographical districts. Lower Bucks revolves around industry and entertainment; Central Bucks, arts and government. Upper Bucks revolves around its rural self, offers outstanding natural beauty and outdoor recreation, and is more tied to Manhattan and the Lehigh Valley than to Philadelphia.

Open spaces in the southern part often house conference centers; in the northern part, summer camps are more likely.

Scenic beauty at places like Ringing Rocks County Park attracts visitors to the northern end.

The intense growth of the county in the last half century — the population jumped from 308,567 in 1960 to 625,249 in 2010 — has produced an entire layer of newcomers drawn to this place by its name and fame. Many know little about the towns they have settled in and don't "get" the big picture at all. The busy-ness of twenty-first century life keeps them more or less in their own neighborhoods and they don't venture off to explore this wondrous place, to uncover its secrets.

I've written this book for them, for tourists who want to know more about the places they visit, for my family, for my friends — and for myself.

Join us on this journey as we skip through history to find today.

THE LIFE-GIVING DELAWARE

The Delaware River, far below the Nockamixon Cliffs, winds through the hills.

The role of the Delaware River, which borders the county's eastern edge, is truly a defining one. It not only separates much of eastern Pennsylvania, including Bucks County, from New Jersey, it also has been a major factor in much of the county's history and growth.

It is the longest free-flowing river east of the Mississippi; its waters travel 330 miles from their source in New York's Catskill Mountains to the mouth of Delaware Bay where they disappear into the Atlantic Ocean. The Delaware provides water for more than 15 million people, including Pennsylvania and New York City residents.

Geologists tell us it is a young river working furiously to cut into the rock beneath. Sometimes its calm waters mirror its surroundings, but they can be angry and unruly, racing wildly up riverbanks, flooding whole towns and wiping out bridges.

The Delaware is not navigable north of the Falls of the Delaware, now Morrisville, where it tumbles down the rocky ledges from the Piedmont Plateau onto the lower coastal plain.

The falls helped to confine growth to the lower end of the county when the Industrial Revolution turned farms into factories. For industry, the river has been a source of both power and shipping. North of the falls, it offers excellent fishing and boating.

The early colonists turned to the river for water, for food — fish, especially shad, was plentiful — and even for shelter. Those early Quakers who had sailed from England only to arrive in cold weather often sought natural caves

1: The river is much wider near the Bristol Wharf where a fisherman tries his luck.

2: Sunbeams sparkle off the water on a clear autumn day at Andalusia.

along the riverbank to shield them from winter's wrath. The river was the main source of transportation for the early colonists, just as it had always been for the Lenapes, who had lived here for thousands of years and called themselves the Original People.

The Lenapes traveled by dugout canoe and tended to build their villages along the river flats as well as on the banks of the larger tributaries such as the Neshaminy Creek.

It was far easier to navigate a boat through river and creek than it was to follow narrow native paths or cut a trail through the woodsy wilderness. Even William Penn, when he visited Pennsbury Manor, his country home in Bucks, traveled by barge from Philadelphia.

The Delaware also was the main source of water for the pioneers' commercial use. The Quakers, the first to settle here, snatched up the fertile, best lands along the river. Early villages grew up along the banks of the river and streams.

The Germans, who arrived thirty to fifty years after the English, were left with second-best land. Even so, that land west of the river still offered exceptionally good soils, and the settlers were wise and careful farmers. Their inland farms, which drew water from nearby creeks, the great river's tributaries, prospered.

Settlers built mills along the creeks, and villages began to form around them in the eighteenth century. Sturdy Durham boats built in what is now the county's northernmost riverside township took iron and produce to Philadelphia in the 1700s. Two centuries later the

process was reversed, when ocean-going vessels carried iron ore from other countries up the river to U.S. Steel's giant Fairless Works just north of Pennsbury Manor.

In the 1800s, seeking the river's beauty and its cooling breezes, wealthy Philadelphia families built their summer homes on the banks of the Delaware in Bensalem, the township closest to the city. Andalusia, home of the Biddle dynasty and now a house museum still owned by the family, had its own wharf where excursion steamboats deposited and retrieved their guests.

Passengers included the less privileged who would escape the city's heat at nearby parks. The paddle wheel boats ran daily excursions from Philadelphia to Bristol, the county's oldest town, where Victorian mansions climbed the steep riverbank and pleasure boats sailed the river.

My grandfather, Daniel W. Gorman of Bristol, who died before I was born, was an engineer on the steamship, *S. S. Columbia*, one of the party boats that cruised the Delaware from Philadelphia to Bristol.

It was supposedly the most elegant of the steamships, had the most enclosed space, and offered the best moonlight cruises with a full orchestra on board. But it served the country as well. During World War 1, moored in Philadelphia, it was used as a floating boarding house for dockworkers.

River islands, formed of rocks and soils deposited by glaciers, attract migrating waterfowl and songbirds as well as fishermen and boaters. Lewis Island, which lies between New Hope and Lambertville, New Jersey, is home to the only remaining licensed shad fishery on the Delaware.

During World War I, a giant shipyard along the river at Bristol turned out ships at an amazing pace. In World War II, the yard was converted to a plant that built airplane parts.

The portion of the river lying above the falls, while not navigable, has always offered recreation. Today, sightseers can cruise a scenic Delaware aboard the River Otter, a pontoon boat, based in Upper Black Eddy. The river still offers good fishing and fun for small boats and jet skis.

The snow-covered River Road curves past the Nockamixon Cliffs.

PENN'S LEGACY
ENDURES

Pennsylvania's founder William Penn was an idealist and a deeply religious man; he was also pragmatic and wise. To feel the pulse of Bucks County, one must first consider Penn's story and his legacy.

Penn threw off the trappings of life as a wealthy English aristocrat and left the Church of England to embrace the teachings of the Society of Friends, a new religion, one strong enough to challenge the crown and frequently send its outspoken supporters to jail.

Penn's Holy Experiment came to life in the late 1600s. The people Penn welcomed to his new world were victims of war, persecution by church or state, poverty, or all of those combined. Many of them were wealthy men who brought their families with them to seek freedom of mind in a new world.

Members of the Society of Friends, also called Quakers, set sail from England to settle here even before Penn came to claim land he had been granted by Charles II in lieu of a debt the king owed Penn's late father.

Penn's province covered 40,000 square miles, equaling the combined mass of Ireland and Wales, and stretched from what is now the Mason-Dixon line, along Pennsylvania's southern border, to New York State.

Penn was Pennsylvania's first governor, but he was also its first real estate developer. Although the Quakers were among the first settlers, Penn's colony was open to everyone.

Fifty or so years after the Quakers, came the Germans, from the embattled Palatinate where warring princes tore through the countryside. At about the same time, the Irish and Scots fled both poverty and an unforgiving British crown. An Irish Catholic settlement grew along Haycock Run in the northern part of Bucks County and Scots and Irish Presbyterians settled in what

is now Bedminster Township. The Germans took over much of the northern lands.

Penn's offer of freedom of religion drew other dissenters — Moravians, Mennonites, and Dunkards. These sects, as well as Catholics, were not welcome in other places; for much of the eighteenth century, Pennsylvania was the only colony where Catholics were allowed to worship in public, and Jews and free blacks walked the streets without fear.

Penn, probably influenced by his earlier imprisonment in the Tower of London, set up a democratic form of government. Jailed four times between 1667 and 1671, he believed in reform rather than punishment, calling for workhouses rather than dungeons, allowing bail for all crimes except treason and murder, and limiting the death penalty to those two acts, a huge departure from

1: Pennsbury Manor is beautiful even in March.

2: A reproduction of William Penn's launch is housed at the restored plantation.

3: Hannah Penn served tea in the best parlor. She was Penn's second wife.

4: Small outbuildings line the path toward the house.

My family went to Pennsbury often when I was a child. I raced around the lawn and romped through the restored manor house before it was furnished. Having grown up in Penn's shadow, as it were, I was stunned when I first visited Oxford University. There in one of its great halls was a portrait of William Penn as a young man — a soldier in a suit of armor.

I had always connected him with peace. I learned that he had served in the military in Ireland as a young man before he became a member of the Society of Friends.

I think it meant even more to me when I realized he knew what horrors armed conflict could bring and he had turned away from it to follow a peaceful path. Still, he went bravely to jail rather than compromise his beliefs.

the English system, where two hundred crimes bore hanging sentences. Thomas Jefferson called Penn "the greatest law-giver the world has produced."

Penn encouraged Quakers to give women full membership rights and equal participation in all functions of the religion. The women of the Society of Friends were, and still are, notoriously outspoken.

Penn treated the native Lenape tribes with respect, learned their language, paid them for their land and feasted with them.

On a more personal level, Penn, although he planned the City of Philadelphia, was essentially a farmer, who believed the country offered a healthier environment than the city.

He sailed the Delaware on his barge, roamed these dense woods and rolling hills, entertained the Lenapes at his home and worshipped with our ancestors in a meetinghouse in Fallsington. He did not strictly follow the Quaker tenets; for example, his dress was more ornate, but it was still simpler than that of his fellow aristocrats. His home was more elegant than plain.

It is not possible to either live in or visit Bucks County without thinking of Penn. This is the founder's county. Even though business abroad allowed him to spend little time here, his footprints are everywhere and they are large. His legacy endures.

BIG STEEL'S DRAMATIC ENTRANCE

Decades before the steel company arrived, the entrance to a lime kiln at the long gone Durham Iron Works furnace was rebuilt.

1: The letters on this old tombstone probably marked the passing of a Pemberton child.

2: Once Levittowners settled in, their families grew — and so did their houses.

The decade between 1950 and 1960 brought a dramatic and sudden end to the Bucks County I knew as a child.

Bristol and most of the other small towns and villages in Lower Bucks County were surrounded by farms when I was growing up. Many, including two large commercial operations owned by the King and Starkey families, had prospered during World War II. The 6,500-acre King Farms was the largest vegetable farm east of the Mississippi and marketed as far west as Chicago. Many of the nine hundred seasonal workers were Haitians who lived in small cabins on the farm. They rode by the truckload past our house.

In 1950, the giant United States Steel Corporation swooped into Bucks, plopped down more than $4 million, and swept up 3,800 acres of fine fields close to the land William Penn had chosen for his country home centuries earlier. Big Steel is said to have paid an average of $1,300 an acre for its riverside property between Bristol and Morrisville.

The company needed access to the river for giant ore boats to dock, and it is ironic that it chose to buy the fine farmland so prized by the first Quakers. About fifty families, many of whom were descendants of the original settlers, were involved in the sale of the property.

When the land changed hands, the remains from two Quaker graveyards were moved to the nearby Fallsington Friends Cemetery. And the graves from an old cemetery on the Starkey property where Penn's land agent, Phineas Pemberton and his family, had been buried, were moved to Pennsbury Manor.

All this happened very quickly — a farming culture was wiped away in months and replaced by an industrial one. For those residents who had always expected Bucks County to remain the way it was, the development came as a devastating blow. In a single decade, the coming of the mill doubled the county's population and, in the lower end, changed its character from rural to suburban/urban.

The onset of the Korean War in June 1950 increased the country's demand for steel, and ground was broken for the huge steel plant on March 1, 1951. The Fairless Works, named for Benjamin F. Fairless, the company's president at the time, was built with unaccustomed speed, and began operations in December 1952.

The plant included a steel mill, blast furnaces, open hearth furnaces, coke batteries, strip, rolling and pipe mills, sheet and tin departments and a vessel slip. At its height in 1974, it employed more than 8,000 workers.

The arrival of the Fairless Works drew other industries and businesses to the lower part of the county and gave birth to two new communities constructed to house workers.

One was the brainchild of John W. Galbreath, an Ohio realtor, whose Danherst Corporation started construction of the 5,000-home Fairless Hills community in April 1951.

Within a year, mega-builder William J. Levitt & Sons, of New York, began work on an 18,000-home project the builder named after himself. It covered five municipalities who had to re-invent themselves to deal with the expansion.

Levitt turned out 180 houses a week with construction tasks tightly defined, some workers performing only a single twenty-minute job in each house. Others worked in teams. With painters, for example, one team used only white paint, another only black. Interestingly enough, both companies made their headquarters in historic mansions and left them standing in the middle of the new suburbia.

Most of the steel plant was shut down in 1991, but other companies now occupy portions of the property and employ local workers. A Spanish firm, Gamesa, manufactures wind turbines there, but even combined, the work forces don't match U.S. Steel's numbers.

Despite dire predictions, both Fairless Hills and Levittown have survived and thrived. The residents worked hard, reared their children, sent them off to college or career, and some of those children bought homes in Levittown. Many families who could have moved on to larger homes chose to stay. Some even returned after moving away. Most either improved or enlarged their properties over the years, and the neat tree-lined communities for the most part remain pleasant.

TWO MANSIONS
STILL STAND

Three Arches was built on the site of a 1684 log cabin. The arched stone section was added after 1762.

Two old stone mansions, surrounded by tall trees and built over the course of centuries survive as symbols of Old Bucks County in the midst of miles of twentieth century development homes.

Standing proud and tall on Trenton Road, which runs through Fairless Hills, is Three Arches, and tucked away on curving Holly Drive in Levittown is the home now known as the Bolton Mansion. Both are listed on the National Register of Historic Places.

Three Arches can be traced back to 1684, when a farmer named Thomas Atkinson and his wife, Jane, built a log cabin on the site.

The 156-acre farm later passed through several hands and the first stone section of the house, placed on the original cabin foundation, was built sometime after 1712 when John and Mary Sotcher, who had been caretakers at Pennsbury Manor, bought the farm. A descendant of theirs, John Brown, built the arched addition after 1762. The Sotchers were married at Pennsbury Manor, now a popular place for weddings.

Other early families lived at Three Arches until it was sold to the Danherst Corporation in 1951, and the company used it as headquarters while masterminding the construction of Fairless Hills. In 1967, Danherst deeded the property to Bucks County. It is now owned by Three Arches Incorporated, which is raising funds for the building's preservation.

Bolton Mansion, home of Phineas Pemberton, Penn's friend and land agent, was built in stages about a hundred years apart. It was named after the town of Bolton near the Lancashire village where Pemberton was born.

Pemberton's 1687 home is now the rear wing of the main fieldstone house completed by Pemberton descendants in 1790. Now, architects say, the house is a late Georgian country mansion and shows some aspects of the Neo-Classical style that was becoming popular at the time. It contains twenty-seven rooms that have been rebuilt and renovated over the years.

In addition to Pemberton's activities with William Penn, he was a member of Penn's provincial council and served as speaker of the state assembly. In Bucks County, he was register of wills, recorder and clerk of the courts.

Through marriage, the property was transferred to the Morris family, wealthy Philadelphia Quakers. They had ties to the University of Pennsylvania which used the property as an experimental farm for about one hundred years. The Morrises gave the farm to the University of Pennsylvania in 1938.

United States Steel purchased Bolton Farm in the late 1940s for executives planning the construction of the nearby Fairless Works.

William Levitt bought the house and constructed Levittown around it in 1952. He later gave the property to Bristol Township. It is now owned by the Friends of Bolton Mansion Inc., which is researching the complicated histories of the various structures and renovations incorporated into the mansion and raising funds for its restoration.

The wharf at Bristol was the busiest place in town for centuries; today it's a park.

Bristol's population is diverse enough to have made William Penn's heart swell with an un-Quakerish pride; he welcomed all to his New World and they certainly came to Bristol.

You can read their presence in the statues in Bristol Lions Park along the waterfront. First, in the 1990s, the Italian-Americans erected a bust of Christopher Columbus. A few years later a Celtic cross rose to honor the Irish, Scots, and British from southwest England who settled in Bristol.

The Hispanic community then built a monument featuring a Puerto Rican watchtower and the African-Americans erected a statue of Harriet Tubman, the abolitionist slave who repeatedly made dangerous Underground Railroad trips.

The Borough of Bristol, well into its fourth century, is a shining example of survivorship.

Quakers founded the town in 1681, calling it Buckingham at first in honor of Penn's British holdings, and it still is the center of the industrial southern end. The once tiny riverside town grew up around a ferry and a mill and barely survived a great fire in 1724. It wiped out most of the early buildings.

Later, the town had to overcome divided allegiances when passions ran high before the Revolutionary War. Both American and British troops walked its streets. In 1757, the town played unwilling host to the king's men, two hundred of whom were billeted in individual homes. When the county commissioners were billed for their expenses, they refused to pay and the town was stuck with the bill.

In 1776, patriots actually destroyed the original St. James Episcopal Church, because they thought it too emblematic of the King. A Church of England missionary, a former Quaker himself, had swayed the founding Quakers to his faith and Queen Anne had sent a solid silver communion service to the church when it was built in 1712. The patriots chased away the rector and church members and for a while American cavalry troops stabled their horses in the ruins.

Just two blocks away, the British took over Bristol Friends Meeting during the war and used it as a hospital. Built In 1711 with bricks sent from England, it had survived the Great Fire and is the oldest building in town.

American General John Cadwalader headquartered his troops at Bristol's King George II Inn while he awaited orders from Washington. Built in 1765 and once known as the oldest inn in continuous operation in the country, it was closed for a short time several years ago, but has since reopened.

The popularity of the Bristol Spa, where people bathed in mineral waters in the 1780s to 1820s, brought an aristocratic crowd and a sparkling social life to the mansions along Radcliffe Street. A Spanish ambassador lived there and Joseph Bonaparte, Napoleon's brother and former King of Spain, was a frequent visitor.

Thomas Cooper, a famous British actor, lived on Radcliffe Street in a house he had won in a game of cards in Paris. He liked to party and his children tended to interfere with his entertaining, so he built an additional riverside home for them and their governess. His daughter, Priscilla, married Robert Tyler, son of President John Tyler.

The town's economy also benefited from an energetic crew of shipbuilders. The arrival of the Delaware Division of the Pennsylvania Canal and the coming of the Pennsylvania Railroad in 1834 turned Bristol into a busy transportation hub.

The town continued to survive the rise and fall of economic tides as the Industrial Revolution brought more change, and later, when workers were needed for war production — and then, when peace arrived, not needed.

Prosperity shifted back and forth as workers carried their lunch buckets to woolen, lumber and carpet mills in the nineteenth and early twentieth centuries, built Liberty ships during World War I, airplane parts during World War II and traveled to the nearby U.S. Steel plant during the Korean War.

The powerful Joseph Ridgway Grundy, who died in 1961 at the age of 98, was the town's first citizen. A former United States senator, Republican Party kingmaker and mill owner, he gave the town land, borough hall and the sycamores lining the streets, but, at the same time fought child-labor laws and workers compensation. The first floor and stairway of Grundy's mansion look like the interior of a sailing ship. Bristol was a shipbuilders' town. The bachelor Grundy and his sister lived there until their deaths. It is now the Margaret R. Grundy Memorial Museum.

Old-timers claimed Grundy hid children under peach baskets to spy on his workers, and that may be so, but today the Grundy Foundation has built a museum, a library, housing for seniors, a skating rink, and other projects in Bristol and throughout the county.

Grundy employed the Irish in his woolen mill where the town clock tower still stands, later imported Italian workers and built them sturdy row houses with Old World-style columned porches.

With World War II came an influx of Polish and Czech workers who fled Pennsylvania's Coal Region to work in the war plants. Many of these settled in town, and their families remain long after the mills and plants have disappeared.

Bristol is now a modern industrial center and serves as headquarters for several large corporations

1: St. James Episcopal Church and cemetery, burial site of Revolutionary soldiers and colonial celebrities.

2: The sun-filled and serene interior of the Bristol Meetinghouse, built in 1711.

3: The historic King George II Inn survived the coming of both British and American troops.

4: The riverside home of the late Senator Joseph R. Grundy is now a house museum.

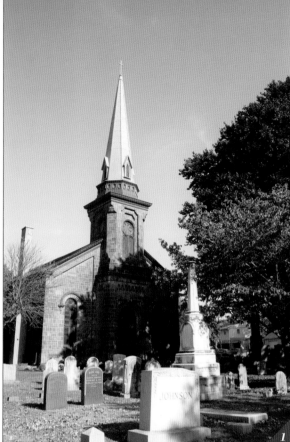

WINDOWS TO THE PAST

The tiny Gallows Hill Cemetery was opened in the 1740s. Buried there are Revolutionary soldiers, colonists, and Native Americans.

Bucks County is truly a genealogical hotspot. Meryl Streep is one of thousands who can trace family roots to Bucks County. The Academy Award-winning actress visited Wrightstown and the Neshaminy Creek in 2010 as part of the filming of PBS television's *Faces of America* series.

One of her ancestors, John Wilkinson, settled in Wrightstown in 1713. He was a member of the Wrightstown Friends Meeting until his support for the American Revolution caused his separation from the Quakers. Wilkinson Road is named for the family. Other ancestors, the Crispins, were distant relatives of William Penn.

Bucks County settlers were primarily English, Germans, and Scots-Irish. They squabbled among themselves, but eventually many crossed those cultural blockades, fell in love, and married, creating what was to become a new American culture. Many of their descendants spread that culture westward.

The family of frontiersman Daniel Boone was one of these. He was born in New Britain Township in 1734 before his family moved to Berks County, where they established their homestead. He went on to open the great wilderness road through the Appalachian Mountains leading from North Carolina and Tennessee to Kentucky, a road followed by legions of immigrants moving westward.

Another Bucks Countian was Army Lieutenant Zebulon M. Pike, who discovered Pike's Peak in Colorado in 1806 while determining the southwestern borders of the Louisiana Purchase. He lived in Lumberville.

As the American Frontier opened during the eighteenth and nineteenth centuries, those seeking more open space or broader opportunities, as well as people prodded by the sense of adventure traveled westward, leaving behind the bones of their ancestors. Eventually some of the descendants of those pioneers wanted to know more about their family backgrounds and turned toward their ancestral homes.

Years ago when I was attending a gathering of my husband's extended family in southern Indiana. I met, unbelievably, a distant cousin of the Clark family whose name was Randy Neely.

When he discovered where I lived he told me he was a descendant of the Neely family of the Thompson-Neely House at Washington Crossing Historic Park. Surely, the Bucks County genealogical pool has spread far and wide.

Although people have always shown interest in their beginnings, the trend seemed to escalate after Alex Haley's television series *Roots* explored the histories of black families. The Bicentennial celebrations in 1976 also prompted people to open windows to the past.

Local librarians today continue to be besieged by callers requesting information about ancestors who once lived here. So are those worthy souls who volunteer at local historical societies — practically all of which have compiled detailed histories of early pioneers.

1: The inscription on this tombstone remains clear after more than two centuries.

2: Old tombstones like this make a genealogist's job more difficult.

3: German names mark the tombstones at St. Matthew's Lutheran Church in Bedminster Township.

So have individual family members. The Frankenfield family is one that spread across much of the county. The local history room at James A. Michener Library in Quakertown, for example, has a handsome gold embossed volume titled *Frankenfield Kin & Family Data*.

The details of generations of births, marriages and deaths march in small type across 538 pages, surely rivaling the "begats" listing of generations in the Bible. Like most family histories it was painstakingly prepared and recorded. In this case the Frankenfield descendant had moved away, but she cared enough to continue this remarkable history.

Workers at churches throughout the county also face constant queries from people across the country. Most early families were affiliated with religious groups who tended to keep thorough birth, marriage and burial records. The Quakers, particularly, were very careful with their records and have faithfully maintained them.

A member of the Society of Friends claims this was because the pool of early Quaker families was limited and mostly people married within the church. Before the settlers even knew about the gene pool, they recognized the marriage of close relatives could be responsible for future health problems.

It's not easy to trace early ancestors. Ancient tombstones in Bucks cemeteries often are simple jagged rocks stuck in the ground — some unmarked, some inscribed with one or two initials only and perhaps a date. Local historians believe some of those earliest stones marked the graves of Lenape Indians who had befriended colonists.

Centuries of rough weather have wiped inscriptions off many of the older tomb stones; nevertheless, the families are memorialized, perhaps unintentionally, in a different way — with neighboring roads still bearing the names of the farmers who drove their wagons over them.

In the northern part of the county, where most of the settlers had come from Germany, the inscriptions on some stones were cut in the fanciful script of Old High German.

THE CROSSING — AGAIN AND AGAIN

The advance guard boards the first of four Durham boats.

What happened December 25, 1776, truly is an American Christmas story. It began in Bucks County and, thanks to an actor, is still celebrated here.

The future of an embattled and struggling young nation hung in the balance, and against all odds, a general saw his men safely across an icy river to New Jersey, marching them nine miles through sleet, freezing rain and snow to victory.

The Crossing, an event dear to the heart of Bucks Countians, is celebrated every year at Washington Crossing Historic Park.

Today high water, swift currents and insurance issues have occasionally caused the cancellation of an actual crossing during the annual re-enactment, but nothing, neither an ice-clogged river nor cold and weary ill-clothed soldiers, stopped General George Washington as he led his troops to Trenton.

Washington's defeat of the Hessians stationed there has been called the turning point of the War of Independence. The re-enactment takes place near McKonkey Ferry Tavern in the 500-acre park.

The first re-enactment was staged sixty years ago by the flamboyant St. John Terrell, an actor and master showman, who had earlier founded the Bucks County Playhouse and the Lambertville Music Circus across the river. Terrell donned tri-corn hat and cape and portrayed Washington every year until 1978, when he passed the coveted role on to others.

The Christmas Day re-enactment and an earlier dress rehearsal are inspiring events, which truly bring history to life, drawing thousands of spectators of all ages.

I've watched the re-enactment several times, always on Christmas Day with my family, and it's usually bitter cold and windy down by the river. But it's not the cold that makes me shiver; it's more the sense that this thing really happened here, that these were real people, ancestors of people I know. Even though called a rag-tag army, they were driven as a group by some cause greater than themselves, greater than their own fears and discomforts.

I watch the gray river wrap itself around the first boat and I think of the men on that frozen trek to Trenton. What they accomplished was truly awe-inspiring. They surprised the Hessians, won the battle and took about nine hundred prisoners. No American troops were killed in the battle.

I think also of Captain James Moore and the men who died not from the effects of the Battle of Trenton, but from previous wounds, from disease and exposure, and whose sacrifice is remembered in a straight and silent row of unmarked tombstones, American flags flying at their heads, in another part of the park.

Bundled in heavy winter jackets, scarves and gloves, they either line the riverbanks in Pennsylvania and New Jersey or peer down from a bridge as Durham boats carry the troops to New Jersey. Visitors come from all over the world. In 2010, we chatted with a family from Thailand.

The boats are manned by Colonel John Glover's Marblehead Regiment, all Massachusetts fishermen. Washington had employed the proud sailors with the red voyager caps before and he knew he needed their skills to navigate the treacherous river. In 1776, the Marbleheaders, who had traveled with Washington, ferried all his troops across the Delaware and marched to Trenton.

They fought in the surprise attack, and made the return crossing with the army and 900 Hessian prisoners in just thirty-six hours. The Marbleheaders brought back only four American wounded, including a nephew of Washington's and James Monroe, the young lieutenant who was to become president.

General Washington (second from right) and his officers march to the riverbank.

The original crossing involved 2,400 troops, eighteen cannons, fifty to seventy-five horses, and baggage. Now four Durham boats, replicas of those commandeered along the river, carry about 160 re-enactors. Washington is the only historical character who is identified. All others are volunteers who serve as unnamed officers or troops.

Even if river conditions prevent an actual crossing, the activities include everything except an actual launching, and spectators can watch military drills and ceremonies on the river bank.

1: Red-capped Marbleheaders carry oars to the launching point.

2: Oars up, the troops get ready to follow the previous boat.

3: A boat heads toward the riverbank on the New Jersey side of the Delaware.

HIGH SOCIETY IN BENSALEM

The splendid Andalusia, one of eighteen estates that once lined the Delaware River, is now a house museum.

Once upon a time eighteen magical mansions lined the banks of the Delaware River in Bensalem Township, the glow of candles and the sounds of music and laughter spilling out over the river during evening festivities. That still happens today at two of the mansions that host weddings and parties.

Most of the mansions were summer homes built for Philadelphia gentry who wanted to escape the city's heat.

Some have been torn down. Some have had their lush lawns paved over as industrial parking lots. Others, privately owned, still exist. Only one, though, Andalusia, has been preserved as a house museum and is open to the public by appointment.

For close to two hundred years the estate has been owned by the wealthy and influential Biddles of Philadelphia, a dynasty of patriots, military officers, financiers, bankers, judges, and lawyers. Today, the Greek Revival mansion, which gave its name to the surrounding neighborhood, has become iconic.

Both the mansion and the grounds of the one hundred-acre estate are now used extensively for wedding ceremonies and receptions, private parties and corporate events.

It was Nicholas Biddle who really created Andalusia, the exquisite home overlooking the river. He was a child prodigy who entered the University of Pennsylvania when he was only ten years old. Denied a degree there because of his youth, he transferred to Princeton and graduated in 1801, as valedictorian, when he was fifteen.

Nicholas, a lawyer, editor, and state legislator, ran afoul of President Andrew Jackson after a banking dispute and lost much of his fortune as a result. (The house was actually saved from the auction block in 1865.) However, while Nicholas had his money, he poured it into his beloved Andalusia. He had bought the property from his father-in-law, John Craig, in 1814. It was a 1775 farmhouse converted into an English Regency mansion by Benjamin H. Latrobe, an eminent architect.

Nicholas, who had toured Europe and the Mediterranean, was fascinated by Grecian ruins, and hired Thomas U. Walter, the architect who designed the dome and the House and Senate wings of the U.S. Capitol, to re-design the house.

Walter added rooms and wings and finished the side facing the river with a giant Doric-columned portico copied from a temple in Athens. He left the opposite English Regency exterior intact.

Nicholas and his wife, Jane Craig Biddle, furnished the house in American Empire style. Tours reveal expansive views of the river from the floor-to-ceiling windows of the double parlors, priceless furnishings, and family portraits (copies of Thomas Sully paintings now in museums.) Wedding gifts still there were sent by Joseph Bonaparte, once King of Spain, and the Marquis de Lafayette, both of whom were family friends. Also displayed are ceremonial swords and military awards. The rare books Nicholas collected are still on his library shelves.

The house basically remained unchanged for about sixty years before plumbing was installed in the early twentieth century.

The gardens range from formal to whimsical (one Biddle had a bathtub set amidst the bushes) and offer a changing show of color. Virgin forests at the estate's edge give way to rare specimen trees providing shade. Walkways cut through the lawns dotted with romantic Greek outbuildings, statues and columns.

Nicholas, the ultimate gentleman farmer, bred racehorses, prize-winning Guernsey cattle, and, for a while, silk worms. His farm buildings radiate nineteenth century charm.

Now a National Historic Landmark, Andalusia is open to the public by appointment. Jamie Biddle, who heads the Andalusia Foundation, a non-profit created in 1980, lives at the estate in The Gothic Cottage, built by Nicholas and his wife in 1838 to handle the overflow of summer guests.

The only other riverside mansion open to the public in Bensalem is Andalusia's neighbor, Pen Ryn Mansion/Belle Voir Manor, which once encompassed 250 acres and is now a wedding venue and catering establishment.

The mansion was built in 1744 by Abraham Bickley, a shipping magnate, as his summer home. Benjamin Franklin and Benjamin West, the American painter related to the Bickley's by marriage, were frequent visitors at Pen Ryn and became friends. West painted *Benjamin Franklin Drawing Electricity from the Sky* around 1805.

Philadelphia heiress Lucy Wharton Drexel bought Pen Ryn in 1893. She expanded the mansion, adding an art gallery, library and servants quarters and building a carriage house which is now called Belle Voir. Eventually the estate went the way of many old treasures, but a group of investors bought it in the 1980s, restoring and updating it as a catering facility

A Gentleman's Club

Tucked away for seventy-five years among the estates that lie like a green fringe along the Delaware River in Bensalem Township is what has been called "the oldest continuously existing men's club in the world." Still operating under its ancient rules and still limited to twenty-five members — allowed one guest each — it has to be one of the quaintest old boys' club ever established.

Penn's agent James Logan was among the founders of the 280-year-old club, and George Washington is said to have been a guest--but not a member. The club's elite members still prepare their own food under a set of ancient rules.

Organized in 1732 as the Colony in Schuylkill, the club's name was changed to State in Schuylkill fifty years later. Also called Schuylkill Fishing Company, the original wealthy members fished in Philadelphia's Schuylkill River, hunted in the nearby woods and prepared their own dinners — no servants allowed.

A 1903 article in *West Philadelphia Illustrated* called the club "… a miniature government formed to make war upon the fish and the game of the Schuylkill and its bordering forests." Members claimed the club had negotiated its fishing and fowling rights on the Schuylkill directly with the famous Chief Tammany of the Lenni Lenapes.

The original clubhouse on the Schuylkill River, known as the Castle, was moved in 1937 to Devon, the estate of William B. Chamberlain along the Delaware. Its officers were called governor, lieutenant governor, sheriff and coroner — and still are. It is believed the club still pays its rent with fish.

An article appearing in the *Philadelphia Record* on April 28, 1882, had this to say about the invitation extended to President Chester Arthur: "President Arthur will come to Philadelphia on Monday, roll up his sleeves, put on a linen apron and assist in preparing his own dinner. He will shell peas, broil beefsteak and be bossed by a Philadelphia society man who will act as chief cook and caterer."

The menu that day consisted of planked shad, broiled beefsteak, roasted pig, perch and vegetables, and of course, the devastatingly alcoholic fish house punch, which has been the club's main contribution to society. Although much imitated, the original recipe is still a secret.

Guests are governed by the same rules as members and those rules are never suspended. No pastry. No forks used in cooking. Members and guests wash their own dishes. They were still using the original set in 1882 and may still be doing so. Only today's members and guests would know that — and they're not telling.

1: This Doric temple portico, added to the original farmhouse in the 1830s, faces the river.

2: A carved wooden door adds a hint of mystery to the walled garden at Andalusia.

3: Pen Ryn, built in 1744, is now a catering establishment and wedding destination.

4: Belle Voir, once a carriage house, now is the scene of weddings and parties.

TWO NATIONAL SHRINES

The St. Katharine Drexel Mission Center and Shrine is in Bensalem Township, where the former socialite's work goes on.

At first glance it seems surprising that two national Catholic shrines have sprung from the Quaker soil of Bucks County, but after a little thought, it appears to be a supremely fitting location.

The presence of the shrines, midway between Philadelphia and New York City, certainly dovetails with Pennsylvania's origins as a refuge for those fleeing persecution and injustice. The shrines draw the faithful from not only Bucks County, but also from around the country and the world.

The first is St. Katharine Drexel Mission Center and National Shrine in Bensalem. Although the estate still reflects the substance and style of Philadelphia's Old Money at the time it was built in 1892, the saint herself lived an ascetic life, even mending her own shoes to save money for her missions. She established more than sixty mission schools for blacks and native Americans.

The second is the Polish National Shrine of Our Lady of Czestochowa near Doylestown, its 240-foot tower soaring above its hilltop church and monastery, projecting the fresh hopes of an ancient and embattled country.

Both shrines draw large numbers of tourists of all beliefs from all over the world, and legions of pilgrims visit throughout the year and on Holy Days. Both shrines also play important roles in their respective communities.

Katharine Drexel of Philadelphia's tony Main Line, the woman who was to become a saint, acquired an enormous fortune from her wealthy father. A member of a nineteenth century family of philanthropic movers and shakers, she chose to follow a religious path.

St. Katharine Drexel was one of only eleven women inducted last year into the National Women's Hall of Fame, honored as a missionary who had dedicated her life and fortune to improve the lot of those society overlooked.

Outraged at this country's treatment of native Americans and African Americans, she founded the Sisters of the Blessed Sacrament, a missionary congregation, and built the order's convent in Bensalem in 1891. The Mission Center is new but with its red tile roof matches the handsome Spanish missionary style complex. The saint donated nearly $20 million to the poor during her lifetime.

She opened her first mission school for native Americans in New Mexico in 1894, established and financed more than sixty missions around the United States and Haiti and founded Xavier University of Louisiana. Native American and African-American artifacts are scattered throughout the shrine and include an Apache burden basket near her tomb used to collect the petitions of pilgrims.

Canonized as St. Katharine Drexel by Pope John Paul II in 2000, she is the patron saint of philanthropists and those working for racial justice. She died in 1955 at the age of 96 and her body is entombed in a crypt beneath St. Elizabeth Chapel on the 56-acre estate.

The seed of what was to become the National Shrine of Our Lady of Czestochowa was planted on a small farm near Doylestown when a Polish priest converted a barn into a chapel in 1955, echoing the creation of the centuries-old shrine of Jasna Gora in Poland, which also grew from a small wooden chapel.

In 1966, the barn's successor, the handsome American shrine on Beacon Hill overlooking Peace Valley, was dedicated in the presence of President Lyndon B. Johnson, Philadelphia Archbishop John Krol and 100,000 pilgrims.

Its dedication coincided with Poland's celebration of 1,000 years of Christianity. The tall stained glass windows in the main church illustrate the history of Christianity in both Poland and the United States.

Focal point at the shrine is a copy of an image of Mary holding the Christ Child and known as the Black Madonna, said to have been painted by Saint Luke the Evangelist on a tabletop built by Jesus. It holds great meaning for devout Polish people. The Monks of St. Paul the Hermit have guarded the original since 1382 at Jasna Gora. Now known as the Pauline Fathers, they operate the American shrine.

Each August thousands of the faithful join a four-day pilgrimage, walking fifty-six miles from a church in Great Meadows, New Jersey, and camping out at night, before attending Sunday Mass at the shrine. This year marks the twenty-fifth walking pilgrimage.

1: Pilgrims leave their petitions in the Apache burden basket hanging near the saint's tomb.

2: The National Shrine of Our Lady of Czestochowa on Beacon Hill towers over New Britain Township.

3: A pilgrim prays in the Candle Chapel before a replica of the Black Madonna.

FROM ESTATE TO PUBLIC PARK

Neshaminy State Park is a perfect place for Civil War re-enactors to gather before their mock battles.

1: Boats are docked in the marina where the Neshaminy
Creek meets the Delaware River.

2: With their weapons stacked, soldiers enjoy a little
nineteenth century downtime.

In this twenty-first century, the Philadelphia Eagles are leaving their giant footprints on land that was one of William Penn's earliest purchases from the Lenni Lenapes.

Eagles Forest, a six-and-a-half-acre site at Neshaminy State Park, was dedicated in 2008, and park workers and volunteers planted 1,200 trees and shrubs there to try to offset the team's carbon footprint and to restore tree cover to the region. The edge of the forest is close enough to Philadelphia to see the city's skyline.

Today ordinary people, too, leave footprints at the Bensalem park. It encompasses land that was once a great estate called Sarobia along the Delaware River and an important part of the county's earliest history.

Visitors can follow the River Walk either to explore the tidal marsh or watch boaters on the Delaware. They can fish in either the river or the Neshaminy Creek for bass or catfish, swim in the pool, and picnic in one of the pavilions or follow the tree-lined Logan Walk. They can launch their motorboats at the marina where some small yachts still anchor.

Dunks Ferry Road, the 339-acre park's eastern boundary, is one of the oldest roads in Pennsylvania. It led to a Delaware River ferry operated by Dunken Williams as early as 1679.

Part of the park now is composed of the 175 acres of Sarobia when it was owned by Robert Logan, a descendant of James Logan, Penn's colonial secretary. Robert Logan, husband of Sara Wetherill Logan, died in 1956, leaving the estate to the commonwealth. One especially interesting part of the estate, reminiscent of the great English country houses, was an outdoor chessboard where guests served as chess pieces.

The Logans were gentle, caring, generous people, according to a 1937 article in *TIME* magazine, but neither were exactly mainstream thinkers. Logan was president of the American Anti-Vivisection Society, an animal advocacy group that continues to oppose the use of animals in experiments. It's said Mr. Logan did not even like his guests swatting at mosquitoes.

A member of the Theosophical Society had advised Sara Logan to try an experiment in character-building and discharge her servants. Consequently, unlike other wealthy matrons, she hired only kitchen help and the Logans and their guests tended to the rest of the house. Logan liked the estate's grounds kept as close to natural as possible and had only a small outside staff. In addition to the mansion, the estate included a guest house, and twelve other houses and cabins where they allowed poor poets and artists to live.

A guest who made frequent visits to Sarobia was the Hindu philosopher, Jiddu Krishnamurti, who stayed for weeks at a time and presided at discussions. Sarobia was demolished before the park was open to the public.

The park is a busy place and is the scene of annual Civil War re-enactments. Last year's theme was the Appomattox Campaign of 1865 with about 1,000 re-enactors doing battle as well as providing glimpses of nineteenth century downtime in their respective camps.

A VILLAGE TIME FORGOT

Bride and groom trees stand in front of Moon-Williamson House, circa 1685, one of the earliest pioneer cabins in Pennsylvania.

1: The Burges-Lippincott House on Meetinghouse Square was built around 1768.

2: The Quakers built this 1758 stone house for the village schoolmaster.

3: The two-story, stone, 1799 Stagecoach Tavern served drinks until Prohibition began.

Fallsington is called "the village that time forgot." Ironically, it not only is remembered, but also has been restored by its sons and daughters. Perhaps a less poetic, but more appropriate, slogan would be "the village rescued from developers."

Either way, this village, packing four centuries of Bucks County history into a tiny area, has survived pretty much intact. It is a peaceful island, its spacious Meetinghouse Square shaded by ancient oaks springing from land bought directly from the Lenni Lenapes in the late seventeenth century.

In the last century, Fallsington was snatched away from those who might have leveled it by a group of citizens every bit as feisty as the Quakers who settled the village. In 1953, as the Levitt and Danherst companies tore through the countryside, villagers feared their historic homes would be torn down, their land plowed under to be swallowed by industry, shopping centers, housing developments, and the highways beginning to circle it.

They banned together to form Historic Fallsington Inc. and fought hard to save the village.

The organization raised funds, bought and preserved six historic buildings, and worked with Falls Township officials to protect the historic town.

In 1955, a local ordinance established a historic district — the first in the commonwealth. Six years later the state formalized the rights of local governments to establish historic districts. Today many villages in Bucks County are listed as historic districts and most towns have also set aside neighborhood areas that are historic. They are proud of their town's stories, as they should be, but none quite match the charm of Fallsington, a collection of old buildings where centuries mingle happily under ancient, towering oaks and the neon and noise of the twenty-first century seem not to intrude.

Architects believe the Moon-Williamson House, a log cabin, could have been built in 1685. It is said

to be one of the earliest pioneer cabins in the entire state. One of the Moon descendants, Samuel Moon, owned the house from 1769 to 1803. He was a well-known maker of Windsor chairs. The two ancient sycamores that shade the log cabin were called bride and groom trees.

The lovely Burges-Lippincott House is one of the village focal points. Built in 1768, its first owner was Daniel Burgess of the family who had given the land across the village square for the building of a meetinghouse.

Dr. Henry Lippincott, a family doctor, added the southern wing in the mid- nineteenth century and used it as his office. Its woodwork is strikingly beautiful.

The little town was born of rebels and when its future was threatened centuries later, its citizens rebelled again and saved it.

Tall trees shade the Falls Monthly Meeting of Friends in the center of the village. Today, a descendant of the first Quakers drives his horse and buggy to the meeting on the first Sunday of each month.

An ancestor of my husband was a member of the Society of Friends and worshipped with William Penn at the first Fallsington Meeting. Perhaps this is why there is no place else in the county where the presence of history presses down so heavily on me.

My husband, John Headley Clark, is a direct descendant of Henry Marjorum (now spelled "Margerum") — and there's a Headley Lane in town — as well as Headley grave markers.

That first Henry Margerum, who lived in Cheverell, Wiltshire, England, and his first wife, Elizabeth, arrived in the New World Jan. 2, 1682, aboard the Bristol Merchant. Phineas Pemberton, first clerk of the Bucks County Court, registered their arrival.

Henry bought a 350-acre tract two miles south of Yardley in 1688 and later purchased 281 acres in Falls Township. Early records indicate that he played an active role in the community.

In 1685, he was appointed constable in Falls Township, served on the first grand jury and also held a post called fence viewer, a job requiring inspection of fences to make sure they were sturdy, and solving property line disputes among neighbors.

The Falls Monthly Meeting of Friends recorded Elizabeth's death in 1687. Henry later married Jane Riggs of Burlington, New Jersey, and they had four children. One of them, Richard, built a stone house on the River Road between Morrisville and Yardley in 1762 and lived in it until his death in 1786. Today, the names Margerum and Headley still live on in Bucks and beyond.

A WILDERNESS ESTATE

Visitors approaching Pennsbury Manor see the mansion's rear; Penn arrived at the front, which faces the river.

Today's approach to Pennsbury Manor, William Penn's country estate on the west bank of the Delaware in Bucks County, is a long and pleasant path between stone barn and outbuildings.

Visitors — between 25,000 and 30,000 tour the estate every year — follow the main gravel walkway through shade trees and past small outbuildings as they approach the bake and brew house and turn right to the manor house. What they probably don't realize at first is that they are facing the rear of a building designed to be approached from the river — the way Penn did.

A team of oarsmen would row Pennsylvania's first governor the twenty-six miles up the Delaware River from Philadelphia in his barge. He would follow a straight, tree-lined path from the river and climb the brick steps to the classic brick manor built in a style we now refer to as Georgian.

Penn arrived in Pennsylvania in 1682. He immediately selected 8,400 acres in Bucks along the river for his personal estate, and construction began the following year. He went back to England in 1684, sending long and detailed building instructions to his steward. The house was ready when he returned to this country from 1699 to 1701.

Poor health and politics kept him abroad until his death in 1718 and his estate fell into ruins. His descendants sold the land in 1792; 140 years later the Charles Warner Company, which operated stone quarries nearby, gave the ten acres where the house originally stood to the Commonwealth of Pennsylvania.

Based on Penn's written instructions to his steward and on the manor's original foundations, the home and plantation were reconstructed. Opened to the public in 1939, the estate now covers forty-three acres, close to the original number cleared, and is administered by the Pennsylvania Historical and Museum Commission in cooperation with the Pennsbury Society. The two have turned what was largely a forgotten ruin into a National Historic Landmark.

Like the great English country houses of the times, it was meant to be self-sufficient with its brew house, smoke house and ice house, carpenter's shop, formal gardens, kitchen garden and orchard. Bees brought from England pollinated the fruit trees and provided honey and beeswax, and grape vines were imported from France to establish a vineyard.

The plantation comes alive with a full calendar of events each year that features house tours, costumed workers demonstrating plantation crafts, colonial cooking, gardening and the care of livestock. Special historic events include jury trials, a Quaker wedding and a dramatic candlelit Christmas celebration.

Those who visit on quieter days may sense the spirit of William Penn seeming to linger there, seeking peace after facing bitter political conflicts in England.

When U. S. Steel purchased riverfront land near Penn's estate in 1950; the remains from two Quaker graveyards found there were moved to the nearby Fallsington Friends Cemetery. The bodies in a third old graveyard where Penn's land agent, Phineas Pemberton and his family, had been buried, were exhumed and moved to a tiny, stone-walled cemetery at Pennsbury Manor.

Pemberton's name pops up in most of the early records of Bucks County. But the untold stories of those buried with him are intriguing. Agnes Harrison, Pemberton's wife's grandmother, for example, was 81 when she crossed the Atlantic, a venture harrowing even for the young and strong. Born in England during the reign of Queen Elizabeth I, she died in Bucks at the age of 85.

A Pemberton descendant, whose story has been told, however, by the Historical Society of Pennsylvania, was John Stith Pemberton, the Atlanta chemist who invented Coca-Cola®. All in all, an interesting Quaker family.

Also buried in the tiny cemetery are the remains of a murdered Indian, shot point-blank in the 1750s when Penn's peaceful regard for the natives no longer prevailed, and a Vietnam veteran who worked at the estate and died on site in 1985.

1: This is the river side of the restored mansion at Pennsbury.

2: A costumed carpenter works in the joiner's shop during an open house at Pennsbury.

3: The old gate to the garden is sturdy and strong.

4: One of the old tombstones in the tiny walled burial ground at Pennsbury.

DURHAM— A RURAL RETREAT

A working farm is nestled in the slope of Mine Hill in Durham Township.

One of Durham's favorite sons was a teen-age runaway who became a Revolutionary War general and hero. He was Daniel Morgan, born in Durham Township in the winter of 1736. (Local maps still show the tiny community known as Morgantown at the intersection of Rattlesnake and Stouts Valley roads.)

Daniel was the son of ironmaster James Morgan who was part owner of the Durham Iron Works. He worked for his father but ran away from home when he was seventeen. Two years later, in 1755, he began his military career as a driver of a baggage wagon in an expedition against Fort Duquesne in western Pennsylvania.

Morgan later married and settled on a farm in Clark County, Virginia. At the outbreak of the revolution he recruited the brigade known as Morgan's Riflemen from among the backwoodsmen of Virginia and western Maryland. They became legends at the battles of Stillwater and Cowpens in South Carolina.

Today, Durham Township is a mix of farms, country estates, and homes set among hillside fields, wooded tracts, bubbling creeks, and mountain ridges, making it hard to believe its origins were industrial.

Durham was one of the first company towns in America. A post office existed there in 1723, long before Benjamin Franklin was appointed postmaster general in 1775. Only the post office in Philadelphia is older, according to historians. The Durham post office may have closed when the first furnace was shut down, because even the U.S. Postal Service has no record of its existence, but another one appeared in the mid-nineteenth century.

The production of iron and steel were at the heart of Bucks County's development in the eighteenth century and again in the twentieth.

The Durham Iron Works founded by James Logan, Penn's secretary, and a group of wealthy investors, is probably one of the country's first industries. More than two hundred years later and fifty miles away, U.S. Steel's twentieth century furnaces were blasting, turning out steel during the Korean War. Now both companies are gone.

The charcoal blast furnace in Durham was first fired in 1727, and later produced cannon shot for both the French and Indian and Revolutionary wars. Some people believe the iron works had a role in the production of the Great Chain stretched across the Hudson River at West Point in 1778 to stop British ships from going further upriver.

The Treaty of 1737 that resulted in the infamous Walking Purchase was initiated between whites and Indians in Durham in 1734.

Today, the township, centered by the Village of Durham, a small collection of Victorian homes, and a mill, has a population of about 1,100 spread across 10-square-miles.

The iron works owned all of the Durham Tract until it became a township in 1775, and the separate farms were sold to individuals. The township now has only two streetlights, one on Route 611, which runs next to the canal and is lined with commercial properties, and one in the village.

Durham was settled as early as 1698, probably because of the rich iron deposits in the Durham Hills, said to have been guarded by a tribe of warlike Shawnees.

It was a small forest outpost, removed from activity in the lower end, but an important part of the county's economy. The few people who lived in Durham worked for the iron company. George Taylor, one of the ironmasters, lived in Durham at the time he signed the Declaration of Independence. His home, now privately owned, stands just outside the village.

The furnaces required an acre of wood a day to operate and that wood was turned into charcoal for fuel. By 1789, the charcoal burners had stripped all the trees from the surrounding land and the iron works had no fuel. It lay dormant until the business was rejuvenated in 1848 when

This is one of the nineteenth century buildings in Durham Village. It was once a store.

anthracite coal furnaces were built closer to the Delaware River, operating under various owners until 1908.

All that remains of the original furnace is a rebuilt stone arch cut into a hillside just off the Village Green and adjacent to a grist mill built one hundred years later on the furnace foundation.

Another remnant of the mining days is a huge barn erected before the Revolutionary War. It still stands as a kind of overseas in-your-face protest against taxes levied by the King of England. Now, an architect and his wife have built their home inside the barn walls.

The exact age of the 16,000-square foot barn has never been determined. What is known, though, is that the King had ordered tax paid on all structures longer than one hundred feet. The three-story barn measures exactly ninety-nine feet, eleven inches. It once housed mules and slaves who worked in the mines.

On the Village Green a replica of the Durham boats used to carry Washington's troops across the Delaware reminds visitors Robert Durham first built the boats bearing his name near the mouth of what is now called Cooks Creek. The 40-foot, flat-bottomed boats were used to carry pig iron, stoves, and other items to Philadelphia in peacetime. During the Revolution, the boats carried cannon balls and military supplies to the Continental army in the city. On return trips, crews poled the boats loaded with food and supplies back upstream.

Many Durham boats were manufactured to go west with the pioneers, according to Carol Kuhn, a docent at the Sigal Museum in nearby Easton. She said one of her ancestors, Jacob Jung, had worked in the Durham boat yard. Jung told family members because the pioneers had to cross several rivers, including the Ohio; the boats were equipped with wheels for the overland parts of the journey. The people apparently loaded all their goods into the boats just as they did with Conestoga wagons and headed west.

1: The interior of the Durham grist mill; it operated for 150 years before closing in 1967.

2: This giant stone pre-Revolutionary barn once housed mules used in the mines; an architect restored it and lives there now.

3: A replica of the original Durham boat is displayed on the village green.

PEARL BUCK'S FARM

Bamboo grows in patches here and there throughout Bucks County, but nowhere is its appearance more fitting than at the gravesite of Pearl Sydenstricker Buck, a woman who was as much at home in China as she was here.

Tucked in a small clearing in the woods at Green Hills Farm, which the writer bought in 1934, the grave is marked by a simple granite slab bearing her name in Chinese characters, its austere lines softened by colorful flowers and towering bamboo. She designed the marker herself.

In 1932, Buck won the Pulitzer Prize for Fiction for her novel, *The Good Earth*, and in 1938 was awarded the Nobel Prize for Literature for her books on China. She was the first American woman to capture both.

Today, her 68-acre Green Hills Farm, and its complex of buildings just outside Dublin in Hilltown Township, is a National Historic Landmark, and one of the most beautiful estates in the county. About 20,000 visitors tour the writer's home each year.

The earliest section of the house is a one-story stone summer kitchen believed to have been built prior to the Revolutionary War. A fieldstone section was added before 1825, and Buck continued to add living spaces. With a new welcome center update in 2010, the property now displays four centuries of architectural styles.

This house museum is where Buck and her second husband, Richard Walsh, who also was her publisher, reared their adopted mixed-race family of eleven children, and it is still seems more home than museum.

The rambling house with its handsome paneling, two libraries, and nine fireplaces is also warm and welcoming.

The house remains the way it was it was when the author died in 1973. The furnishings, rugs, and draperies are all things she chose. The impressive libraries remain as memorials of her work.

During the years she lived at the farm, Buck founded the humanitarian organizations now gathered under the name Pearl S. Buck International and headquartered at the farm.

A 2010 biography, *Pearl Buck in China: Journey to the Good Earth*, written by Hilary Spurling, describes the childhood experiences that may have given Pearl Buck her passion to help multi-race children often rejected by society.

Among the younger children in a large missionary family, she was often left to wander alone. The child carried a stick, her biographer writes, to fend off dogs fighting over the bodies of abandoned girl babies and often buried the remains herself. That experience made a lasting impression on her.

Buck was a prolific writer; her name is associated with more than 1,000 published works, including plays and radio and television scripts, but her charities have reached further, improving the lives of more than two million children and families discriminated against due to the circumstances of their birth.

While Buck's influence extends around the world, it also is an important part of the Bucks community. Her children grew up here, romping with friends and inviting them to new movies shown at the Buck home.

Today, the estate hosts weddings, private parties, and corporate and benefit events. Writer's conferences and workshops, even one for children, and book discussions bring life to the estate all year long, and locals visit the gift shop.

THE NOCKAMIXON CLIFFS

An ice-climber secures his ropes on the Nockamixon Cliffs.

Probably one of the most remarkable vistas in Bucks County is framed by the towering Nockamixon Cliffs at a curve in the Delaware River just south of the village of Kintnersville. The base of the cliffs hugs the River Road and the Delaware Canal.

The river is bordered by sharp cliffs as it flows south from Easton, but just south of Kintnersville the cliffs soar to the sky.

The nearly vertical red sandstone and shale cliffs extend for about three miles in the area called The Narrows, running along most of the riverfront of Nockamixon Township and reaching into Bridgeton Township to the south. At The Narrows, the river actually flows west to east. The cliffs are part of the Delaware Canal State Park.

Geologists say the cliffs, also known as the Delaware River Palisades, were formed about 200 million years ago from red sand and mud carried from the northwest by streams and laid down in shallow lakes during the Mesozoic Era, a time when dinosaurs first emerged.

During the era's Triassic Period, blistering hot magma from deep in the earth flowed into the lake beds, heating the sand and shale, making them hard and weather-resistant. In the Jurassic Period, which followed, the softer rock was worn away.

Several sources place the cliffs' height at more than 400 feet, and www.mountainzone.org, claims the cliffs peak at 502 feet above the river, towering over nearby farmland.

Whatever their height, their rugged beauty remains unspoiled and in spring and summer, they are majestic,

1: Snow collects on the Nockamixon Cliffs and remains throughout cold weather.

2: Ice-climbers often work in pairs to conquer the 500-foot high palisades.

3: Ice fishermen have a cold wait at the hole they've drilled in frozen Lake Nockamixon nearby.

their rocky profile broken here and there with waterfalls and gorges spilling water over their sharp ledges. In those seasons, some greenery clusters bravely along cracks in the rocks, including plants found only in Arctic/Alpine habitats and rarely found south of Maine in this country.

In autumn, the foliage is spectacular. President Grover Cleveland, a famous angler, would sneak away from the White House in September and October for a few days of bass fishing in the Palisades shadows with a local guide.

The highest ledges offer nesting places for raptors; eagles, hawks, ospreys and peregrine falcons have been spotted there. These are only a few of the ninety species of birds that find shelter in the cliffs.

Winter brings magic to the cliffs. They face north, getting little direct sunlight, and as the weather turns colder, virtual rivers of ice, frozen in place as they tumble from deep ravines, form what locals describe as "ice palaces." There are nine major streams of ice, three of which are called amphitheaters by ice-climbers, and one is picturesquely named Dead Deer Gully.

Every winter residents can depend on students to toss purple and gold dye, Palisades High School colors, onto a couple of the more reachable ice floes, reminding passersby where the nearby school got its name.

And every winter when the ice is solid, ice-climbers, wearing brightly colored gear, fix their ice screws, adjust their ropes, and climb up that icy stairway to an incredibly gorgeous view from the area called Top Rock.

The climbers travel to Bucks County from all over the East Coast to test their chilly skills at the Palisades.

At one time five houses stood in the hamlet of Narrowsville; now only their crumbling stone foundations can be seen at the base of the cliffs. At the northern end of The Narrows, though, a frame house stands between the canal and river and gets no direct sunlight for most of the winter.

The sun stops touching the house around the middle of November and doesn't return until mid-February.

The cliffs face due north at that spot, and geographers and historians have frequently compared the forgotten village to the English hamlet of Middleham in the Lynn Valley in North Devon, which is also surrounded by steep cliffs that hide the sun.

Just west of the Palisades is the man-made Lake Nockamixon, centerpiece of Nockamixon State Park.

It's a year-round playground and in the winter, skaters take advantage of the lake, and ice fishermen drill holes in the frozen lake and wait for the big ones to bite. Ringing Rocks County Park offers warm weather fun; when struck with a hammer the rocks sound like chimes.

Ringing Rocks County Park offers warm weather fun; when struck with a hammer the rocks sound like chimes.

Old St. John's, dedicated in 1855, is open only two days a year.

The glowing new stained glass windows at St. John the Baptist Roman Catholic Church in Haycock Township, pay tribute to the parish's early days — and to a tiny group of people who made time and a place for religious devotion even in the face of a wilderness filled with dangers at every turn.

One window shows a missionary on horseback racing down a hill. A startling ball of fire rests on a mountaintop, depicting what was a surprisingly early form of social networking.

People from the village the priest was visiting would build a giant bonfire on a high hill to notify those in the next village he would soon be arriving.

Another portrays a green-robed St. Patrick subduing an evil-looking red snake, a not-so-gentle reminder the parish's founders hailed from Ireland, although for years those in the parish were a mixture of Irish and German — and bilingual for the most part. For many years, parishioners had to sit through two sermons, one in English and the same one in German.

But it is the story of a single Irish family, the McCartys, that is inextricably bound to that of the parish.

Edward and Catherine McCanna McCarty were among the first Irish immigrants to take advantage of Penn's Holy Experiment and settle in Bucks County. The McCartys came from County Cork and they probably arrived in 1737, traveling with Edward's parents, Nicholas and Unity, and most likely were fleeing British oppression.

A deed dated April 19, 1738, shows Edward bought land at the foot of Haycock Mountain from Thomas and

One of the stained glass windows in the new church portrays the parish's early history.

Today, Old St. John's is open only on Memorial Day and All Souls Day, when parishioners still light candles for the dead. Standing white and prime on a small hill in the creek valley, it is a surprising jewel box of colors inside. On the altar, the painting of deer drinking from a fountain is especially meaningful, not just as a Biblical image but as a symbol of life in Upper Bucks County where generations of fathers and sons — and sometimes mothers and daughters — have hunted. It still is not unusual to see a deer carcass hanging outside a farmhouse when deer season opens.

The simple church, flanked by weatherworn tombstones, has a special appeal with its hand-carved pews and a rope an usher would yank to give voice to the bell in the belfry.

The bell is silent now but its voice marked both sad and glad passages of nearly a dozen generations.

A window honoring St. Patrick pays tribute to the McCarty family's birthplace.

Richard Penn. McCarty paid thirty-eight pounds of sterling for 250 acres. The property lies on both sides of Haycock Run, which at that point separates Nockamixon and Haycock townships, and McCarty descendants still live near the original homestead. A hillside cemetery was established on the property in 1743, a half-century before a church was built. The oldest grave is that of Unity Casey McCarty, mother of Edward, the pioneer, and dated 1745.

A tiny group of people kept the church alive in the wilderness. The colony's 1757 census listed only twenty-six Catholics over the age of 11 in the entire county.

Edward's son, Nicholas, married Albertina Kohl, the daughter of neighbors. It was the first of many German-Irish marriages among the early McCarty, Kohl, Buck and Haney families. Nicholas was the first boy born at Haycock. Albertina was baptized August 23, 1741, and her name is listed on the oldest known Catholic birth register in America.

Nicholas and Albertina built the McCarty homestead in Nockamixon and reared five daughters and four sons. Their son, Thomas, was among the "flower and pick of the army," and served in George Washington's honor guard.

The McCarty homestead was called the Mass House because it contained a large room where local Catholics could gather when circuit-riding priests visited every few months to celebrate Mass and perform marriages and baptisms. The Mass House, built around 1776, still stands but the McCartys no longer own it.

The first permanent church, St. John the Baptist, often referred to as St. John's Haycock, was built in 1798 on an acre of land along Haycock Run donated by the McCartys.

St. John Neumann, then Bishop of Philadelphia, blessed the cornerstone of what is now Old St. John's in 1854, and a year later blessed the finished church. The saint's signature can be found in the parish records.

The new church, dedicated in 2003, serves families from seven townships and seats 1,000. Its exterior is white, like its pioneer predecessor.

QUAKER LANDMARKS

The handsome Buckingham Friends Meeting, built in 1806, served as a model for many other meetinghouses.

For the most part Quaker meetinghouses in Bucks County are plain but handsome structures built of native stone and surrounded by ancient trees on generous plots of land. Welcome islands of serenity in a frenetic world, they also are a symbol of simplicity and endurance.

That's because many are modeled after the Buckingham Meetinghouse built by the Friends in 1806. The stone building replaced a log building erected on the site in 1768, which, like the Bristol Meeting, was used as a hospital during the Revolutionary War.

Because Buckingham's elegant design became a prototype for American Friends meetings in Bucks and beyond, it's on the National Register of Historic Places. Although modern conveniences have been added, the basic building has remained unchanged since it was built.

The first generations of Quaker immigrants followed the English tradition of men and women meeting together, then while the men saw to business matters, the women were shunted off to a smaller, less attractive place to handle the "business" of weddings and social gatherings.

By the late eighteenth century, the American Quakers were still gathering for worship, but they used a partition to separate the sexes for their individual business meetings. Buckingham was the first Friends' meeting house to incorporate this practice in its building design, the first to be erected in the symmetrically balanced two-celled or "doubled" form, giving the women's side space equal to and as nice as the men's.

Matthias Hutchinson, a Bucks County associate judge and master mason, was in charge of construction and Edward Good of Plumstead was chief carpenter.

Quickly other Friends began to consider this new design for their own meetings. Most of those built from the later eighteenth century into the mid-nineteenth copied Buckingham.

Two earlier Bucks County meetinghouses have a different, but still elegant, appearance. The white brick Bristol Meeting, built in 1711, is simpler in design, but it's still shaded by ancient trees, including a buttonwood that has been growing there before William Penn's arrival. The Richland Friends Meeting was founded near Quakertown in 1710. Quakers, the first to go to the west in Bucks County, had settled there prior to that date. They had come to the area through neighboring Montgomery County. Meetings were held in members' homes until 1723 when a small log meeting was built. The present building, white stucco over stone, was not erected until 1862, but it resembles the Bristol Meeting and is also surrounded by tall trees.

Richland Friends Meeting celebrated Quaker Heritage Day in September 2010, marking three hundred years of Quakers in the town that bears their name.

In addition to honoring their own history, they also celebrated the culture of the Lenni Lenape who lived among them. Legend has it that the Lenapes met with surveyors laying out boundaries for Penn's nearby Manor of Richlands under a great white oak tree that stood near the great oak they revere so much today. The Lenapes taught the Quakers how to farm in what was then the Great Swamp and how to build bark shelters in the wilderness.

The Quakers did not forget their help, nor did the Lenapes forget the Quakers. Years later, after the shameful trickery of the Walking Purchase that eventually led to the Indian Wars, the Lenapes occasionally raided the white man's homes, but never bothered the Quaker families who had treated them fairly.

The Richland Meeting in Quakertown cherishes its ancient Great Oak.

One highlight of the Quakertown celebration was a series of dramatizations of the meetings for worship, including a passionate plea delivered by a costumed actor impersonating Susanna Heath Morris, who, with her husband, Morris Morris, donated the land on which the meetinghouse still stands.

Born in 1682, Susanna married and had twelve children, before she turned to missionary work. Then she had another.

An amazing woman, her missionary zeal took her throughout the colonies. She sailed to Europe three times, surviving several shipwrecks and run-ins with privateers and warships. Considered by many to be a prophet, she fought for women's rights and against slavery, alcohol and tobacco use. She died in Richland in 1755.

During a dramatization, an actor portrays Susannah Heath Morris giving an impassioned speech.

Many children who grew up to fill important posts in Bucks County and in the colonies in general were educated by the early Quakers, who at first conducted classes in their homes. There was a Quaker schoolhouse at Richland Friends as early as 1742. Education for boys and girls was important to the early Quakers and it continues so today.

They have always taught principles of care for others, truthfulness, simplicity, and peaceful resolution of conflicts. There are now three independent Friends schools of varying ages in Bucks County for kindergarten through eighth grade. Buckingham Friends School was founded in 1794; Newtown Friends School in 1948; and United Friends School in Quakertown in 1983, evidence that the Quaker spirit is still strong.

George School, a private coed boarding and day school near Newtown, founded in 1893 for high school students, continues the Quaker traditions.

At the meeting's 300th anniversary, Quaker Donna Berger and Shelley DePaul, a Lenape language specialist, examine a drum.

A NEW WORLD CASTLE

The tiles in the Columbus room show off Mercer's favorite colors.

*U*nlike the Philadelphia millionaires who hired scores of workers to construct their riverside mansions in Bensalem, Doylestown's favorite genius, Henry Chapman Mercer, was a do-it-yourselfer.

Considered a Renaissance man, he built a castle worthy of his reputation, named it Fonthill, lived in it for twenty years, and left it to the Bucks County Historical Society, of which he had been president. Now, tens of thousands of tourists from all over the world visit this unusual building, which Mercer himself called "a castle for the New World."

Mercer, son of a wealthy Doylestown family, was a Harvard graduate with a mind so sharp and broad it encompassed many cultures and many centuries. His curiosity and out-of-the-box thinking was practically endless — leading him into history, archaeology, architecture, anthropology, ceramics, manufacturing, construction, and collecting and preserving antique tools — so many he had to build a museum to contain them. He was a lawyer, too, in a lawyers' town, although he never practiced law.

Of course, it helped that he inherited a large fortune from a favorite aunt just in time to get him going on his various building projects.

Mercer had fallen in love with the castles he had visited in Europe as a young man, so he designed and built his own. He made it his home, a showplace for the handsome tiles he made at the Moravian Pottery and Tile Works and those he collected in Spain and Japan. His private collections of prints and hand-crafted items were purchased all over the world.

1: Mercer's American tiles, made toward the end of his life, depict harvest activities.

2: Mercer's collection of prints climbs the walls and his tiles fill the ceilings.

3: Henry Mercer's concrete castle reaches for the sky.

4: The tile maker's art seems never to stop.

Fonthill was the first of the three structures he built, and now designated as parts of the Mercer Mile in Doylestown. Fonthill and Mercer Museum are owned and administered by the Bucks County Historical Society, and Bucks County owns and operates the pottery.

Mercer and a handful of workers started construction of Fonthill in 1908; it was completed in 1910. A tall structure with towers, chimneys and arches, twisting stairways and railed terraces, it is made of hand-mixed concrete reinforced with iron, has forty-four rooms and two hundred windows. Its architecture is a mind-boggling but happy mix of Medieval, Gothic and Byzantine beauty.

Some tall windows are enormous and shed sunlight in the dark and dreamy castle rooms and others are small and designed in unusual shapes. Otherwise, the castle is lit with bare light bulbs that show glowing filaments. Fonthill has eighteen fireplaces and an untold number of tall columns supporting vaulted ceilings.

All possible surfaces — floors, walls, mantels, ceilings — are covered with textured tiles, glazed and unglazed, bursting with colors, vivid and subdued — a ceramist's dream gone wild. Even at the entry to the castle, where nobles would have normally hung tapestries, Mercer covered an entire wall with a glowing tile mosaic.

Mercer himself, though, spent much of his time in the giant two-story, balcony room he called the saloon, where he kept the objects he loved most.

Although each room in Fonthill is capable of turning mere interest into astonishment, it is the Columbus Room that produces gasps from visitors, momentarily stunned by the profusion of tiles climbing the walls and lining the vaulted ceiling. "Even Henry Mercer himself wondered if he had overdone it a bit here," said Heather Hicks, an education assistant at Fonthill. Nevertheless, visitors cherish that Mercer exuberance.

THE ORIGINAL PEOPLE

This is a carefully researched replica of one of the Lenape villages that dotted the landscape in the early days of Bucks County.

Today, the Lenape, Bucks County's "original people," are emerging from the shadows of history. They are proud of their heritage and beginning to share the secrets of their past. They called themselves Lenape; we called them Delawares — for the river they loved.

There's a new interest in their language — it's actually being taught in several area colleges. The Lenapes were a matriarchal society with much revered "clan mothers," and we know now it is the women who have preserved their language and their culture.

We know now the white man's pronunciation of the name accents the first syllable: We call them Len-up-pee, while they call themselves Luh-nah-pee. Most of their words are accented on the next to last syllable.

Some authorities say William Penn learned the language to speak with the Lenapes without an interpreter. He once wrote, "Their language is lofty, yet narrow, but like the Hebrew; in Signification full, like short-hand in writing: one word serveth for three, and the rest are supplied by the Understanding of the Hearer." He added, "I must say that I know not a language spoken in Europe that hath words of more sweetness or greatness."

An ever-growing fascination with native culture continues to draw people to listen to their legends, to attend powwows and other gatherings.

William Penn loved and respected the Indians. He described the Lenape as "tall, straight, well-built of singular proportion; they tread strong and clever and mostly walk with a lofty chin." He had an amazing relationship with them, never allowing settlers on the land until the Indians agreed to it, even though he did not have to do that.

About twenty years after Penn's death, his sons betrayed the Lenape — and their own father — with the infamous Indian Walk of 1737. The whites used trained runners to grab up more land — about three times as much as the Indians had agreed to — the land one man could walk in a day and a half. It began in Bucks, in Wrightstown, continued north on what is now Route 611 to Ottsville and veered westward onto today's Route 412 and north into the Lehigh Valley, all the way to Robertson Run, near Mauch Chunk, now called Jim Thorpe.

The Lenape lifestyle differed from ours, of course, but in some ways it had its endearing similarities. For example, both Lenape men and women had tattoos — and they loved them, just as so many of us do.

These long-ago people usually had two fireplaces, one inside their wigwams and another outside for warm weather use — not so different from today with the ubiquitous barbecue and summer outdoor kitchen.

When their families outgrew their single wigwams made of bark, they turned them into longhouses, simply two wigwams put together, just as we build additions or move to larger homes as babies arrive.

In July and August, the entire village took off for New Jersey's beaches — just as we do today.

And there were at least three Ivy League Lenapes in the late eighteenth century. Jacob Wooley was the first Lenape to attend Princeton, a member of the Class of 1762. Three others were sent to Princeton by Congress to keep its promise to provide education for children of Lenapes who sided with the colonies in the French and Indian Wars.

John and Thomas Killbuck and George White Eyes, all sons of Lenape chiefs in Ohio, studied at Princeton in the 1780s — at least John did. He was very studious and did well in geography, mathematics and Latin. His brother, who liked to party too much, was dismissed and put to work to learn carpentry on a Bucks County farm.

Today, stone markers follow the "walk." This shameful theft of land from the Lenapes — and the settlers' failure to correct it — set off bloody attacks and reprisals, and the eventual ousting of the natives to the West.

Before that, Indians naturally merged with whites. In the early days, settlers who did not bring their wives, often married Lenape women or at least fathered their children and took responsibility for them. Many Indian and white families prospered.

But when the red men were chased westward, the mixed families who managed to remain here denied their heritage and hid their children, fearing they would be taken away and sent to Indian schools. In those times, mothers and grandmothers passed on the language and culture in secret to their daughters. Until recently, the Lenape culture and language were thought to have disappeared.

The women also were skilled gardeners, basing their planting on the stars. They particularly watched the star cluster we know as the Pleiades or Seven Sisters, a part of the constellation Taurus. When the Pleiades began to fade from the sky at the beginning of May they knew it was time to prepare the soil and plant their seeds; when the cluster appeared again in October, it was time to harvest.

They followed a procedure we call multi-cropping; they called it "the three sisters." They planted corn kernels in small mounds. After the corn sprouted, they placed beans in the same mounds so the vines could climb the cornstalks. Next, they planted squash or pumpkins so their broad leaves formed a canopy, depriving weeds of light and retaining moisture in the soil.

1: A stone marker on Gallows Hill in Springfield Township shows where the walk turned west and north to the Lehigh Valley.

2: A volunteer describes food preparation and outdoor cooking.

ALL ARE WELCOME

Tiny Rock Ridge Chapel was a center of religious life for the farming community in Tinicum Township for a century.

William Penn's seventeenth century concept of religious freedom has driven its roots deep into Bucks County and the idea continues to blossom year by year. Even as clergymen worry about a flagging interest in morality and the hereafter, new churches are planting themselves throughout Penn's Woods. One, Buckingham's Our Lady of Guadalupe Catholic Church, which seats 1,200, was finally dedicated in 2011 after ten years in the planning stages at a cost of $18 million.

Some of the tiny stone or wooden churches of the past built by Lutherans, especially in the north, and by Presbyterians, Methodists, and many other Protestant denominations sprinkled throughout the county, have been replaced by modern buildings serving as a place for prayer as well as community work and recreation. A few of the historic churches are still used for worship.

What's really interesting is the variety of religions in Bucks County. The county is a mirror of America in this sense. Bensalem has the largest concentrations of Mexicans, Guatemalans, Indians, and Koreans, so it's no surprise — well it is a little surprising, still — to find a Buddhist temple peeking out of a patch of woods.

The Mongkoltepmunee shrine is the only one of its kind in the United States.

It is a place for ceremony and meditation for saffron-robed monks from Thailand who arrived in Bensalem nearly thirty years ago, and for about 2,000 Thai Buddhists in the Philadelphia metropolitan area. The temple is gorgeous, an exact replica of a four-story temple in Bangkok, its gold ornamentation shimmering in the sunlight.

It's interesting that three black churches existed in Bucks County nearly a half century before the Emancipation Proclamation was signed. Their congregations were probably a combination of slaves freed by owners and those who had escaped from the South.

The Bethlehem African Methodist Episcopal Church, the first congregation for African-Americans in the county was founded in Langhorne in 1809. It is still active.

The Little Jerusalem African Methodist Episcopal Church was built in 1830 in a community close to the Neshaminy Creek but the congregation was founded twenty years earlier. The building still stands although its members have scattered.

The Mount Gilead Church was built in 1835 on the top of Buckingham Mountain, a hiding place along the Underground Railroad. At one time a little community was established around it. Regular services at the plain but lovely church ceased almost eight decades ago, although a congregation of whites worshipped there for a while.

Every Easter Sunday morning the doors are opened at 5:15 for a traditional sunrise interfaith service. A mixture of whites and blacks, some descendants of the original congregation, return each year for the brief service and a light breakfast.

Deep in the woods of a northern township, East Rockhill, are three stone pyramids, marking the headquarters of the Fraternitas Rosae Crucis, or the Fraternity of the Rosy Cross. The pyramids are aligned from smallest to largest and mark the memorial garden of the spiritual community, the main and oldest of the modern Rosicrucian movements, founded in 1858 by Paschal Beverly Randolph, a friend of Abraham Lincoln. At the time, the Rosicrucians were intertwined with the Masons, although their history dates to the Middle Ages. Benjamin Franklin reportedly was a member of a Rosicrucian group in Paris when he lived there.

The Rosicrucian movement in Bucks County was revived by Reuben Swinburn Clymer. In the memorial garden, which is adjacent to the Church of Illumination, burial sites of cremated remains of members are marked with a rose instead of a tombstone.

Mysticism and a desire for privacy always breed mystery, of course, and rumors have been circulated by the curious about activities on the grounds; nevertheless, the Rosicrucians appear to be gentle and seem to have lived amicably enough with their neighbors for years.

The Bristol Jewish Center was founded in 1904 in a tailor shop on Mill Street by ten men who had escaped pogroms and prejudice in Eastern Europe. It was the first and only synagogue in the county for years, and also the first in the county to have a female rabbi.

Now ten synagogues serve Orthodox, Conservative, Reform and Reconstructionist congregations.

Now, Bucks County has a growing number of mosques, with an estimated 1,000 Muslim families living in the county.

1: A detail from the temple.

2: The Mongkoltepmunee Buddhist Temple is surrounded by woods in Bensalem Township.

3: A stone pyramid rises above a Rosicrucian cemetery in East Rockhill Township.

Summerseat, a Morrisville mansion owned at separate times by two signers of the Declaration of Independence.

Morrisville and Yardley are among the four larger towns along the Delaware River that now are clustered as Landmark Towns and have joined forces in developing their historic backgrounds and tourist potentials. Bristol and New Hope are the others.

All started as tiny settlements built around mills and ferries. Bridges to New Jersey span the Delaware, and the river plays a role in the daily lives of those who live there, but each town has its own strong personality.

Morrisville, opposite the city of Trenton, New Jersey's capital, and known first as Falls of the Delaware, was situated on the overland route between New York and Philadelphia. Because it was, it had the oldest ferry on the river, believed to have operated even before 1675, but it did not exist as a borough until 1804.

The Dutch got to the area first and settled on Biles Island adjacent to town. There also was a tiny settlement of trappers near the falls. John Wood, one of Penn's original Quaker settlers, owned the land on which the borough now stands.

But while the colonists were dancing and partying in the more settled Bristol, the land that is now Morrisville was kept as private estate and farmland. The first mill was built in 1772 and Morrisville eventually became an industrial town.

Wealthy financier Robert Morris, once described as "the pocketbook of the Revolution," built more mills, once owned 2,500 acres in the area, and, years later, died penniless.

In 1765, Philadelphian William Barclay built Summerseat, a Georgian mansion using both stone and brick. Later, it was sold at different times to Robert Morris and George Clymer, both of whom signed the Declaration of Independence, and is the only house in America owned by two such signers. A truly handsome mansion, its woodwork is especially detailed and it stands on a hill caught in a kind of spider web of small roads at the corner of Legion and Hillcrest avenues. It was last used as an administrative building by the Morrisville School District.

Summerseat also was Washington's headquarters for about a week in December 1776 before he moved his troops further north along the river.

Restored in the 1930s, the mansion is now a house museum and home of the Historic Morrisville Society. Although Summerset is open only one day a month, its annual Patriot's Day in June draws crowds.

Also in Morrisville, an outcropping of rock called Greystones marks the starting point of William Penn's first land purchase and treaty with the Lenapes. The town was, at one time, considered a suitable place for the nation's capital, but the idea was eventually discarded.

Just a few miles upriver lies the lovely little town of Yardley, founded by William Yardley who arrived from England in 1682 and settled with his family on five hundred acres he named Prospect Farm just outside the present town.

Within about twenty years the American branch of the family had died and an English relative established a ferry as well as new family roots. The town grew around it and a few industries thrived for a while.

During the Civil War, Yardley was an active Underground Railroad station with hiding places at its hotel (which still stands and now is called the Continental Tavern), in canal warehouses, at the general store, and in a home facing pretty Lake Afton, a mill pond, at the northern end of town.

The wonderful thing about Yardley is that, although buildings have been added and changes certainly made since the late nineteenth century, a visitor still has a distinct feeling he has traveled back in time when he enters town.

Most of the town is part of its historic district and as it never became a manufacturing center such as Morrisville, it retains the appearance of another age. Houses are small and close together and the roads tend to be quite narrow.

Many of the buildings along Main Street that once were homes now house businesses, but they still look like houses with only small signs identifying them.

1: The tiny Victorian Yardley Library is situated on the shore of Lake Afton.

2: The interesting trim sets this house apart from other Victorians that line Yardley's Main Street.

3: Lake Afton is a quiet place just off the intersection of Main Street and Afton Avenue.

TO MARKET,
TO MARKET...

Fresh herbs welcome customers at Nonesuch Farm in Buckingham Township.

In Bucks County, farmers have either been forced out under development pressures or forced to turn their own farms into something they never were. For the most part, the shrinking farm scene has exploded into something entirely new.

Snipes Farm in Morrisville has been in the hands of the same Quaker family since 1848, but what happens there today is far different from its quiet beginnings.

It is one of several old farms that retain agricultural tradition, dust still swirling as tractors plow the fields, even as gates open to crowds seeking entertainment, recreation, and education.

The Snipes are descendants of James and Jane Moon, who settled on a tract of land near what is now Morrisville after their arrival in the colony in 1682. Their grandson, another James Moon, began to grow and sell ornamental trees there in 1767.

Eighty years later his intermingled Snipes and Moon descendants moved to what is now the Snipes Farm, continuing the ornamental tree business and planting specimen trees that became national champions. Many old estates surrounding New York City and Philadelphia are lined with trees grown from Moon nursery stock.

In the 1950s Brad and Sam Snipes took over the farm, revived the tree nursery, started growing fruits and vegetables, opened a retail store, and wound up with one of the top garden centers in the nation. Within a decade, they had added a driving range, minigolf and pitch-and-putt course.

Now that once peaceful farm, an enduring patch of green with its ancient trees and gorgeous orchards,

Golf courses and a driving range now occupy land the Snipes family once farmed.

is an absolute beehive of activity, offering 150 acres of recreation and entertainment in addition to fresh produce. Susan Snipes-Wells and her brother, Jonathan Snipes, manage the farm. An important part of the farm is the education center, which stresses sustainable agriculture.

Having joined the ranks of those in agri-tourism, the property still maintains a down-on-the farm ambience while hosting corporate events (accommodating up to 2,000), wedding receptions, and family reunions.

Wherever you are in Bucks County during the warmer months you're probably only a stone's throw away from fresh produce and eggs collected that morning. Farm-to-table is no new concept here. At many farm markets you can pick your own fruits and vegetables and a lot of people choose to toil in the sun — the goodies are less expensive, you can purchase the exact quantity you need and the getting down and dirty in the dust is fun for a bit for adults and children.

Then as the seasons change, you can select your own pumpkins right from the fields; find fresh farm-grown turkeys for Thanksgiving dinner and, when snow is in the air, take home a freshly cut Christmas tree.

It's pretty much always been that way in Bucks. Now, the county is home to an astonishing number of farm markets. More than seventy of them dot the roads with baskets and crates overflowing with vegetables freshly pulled from the soil and fruits sun-ripened in orchards.

Some independently owned farms now are known as CSA farms, denoting community-supported agriculture, selling subscriptions that offer weekly shares of seasonal produce. An annual fee is attached and members must commit to provide several hours of labor at the farm during the season.

As members of The Bucks County Foodshed Alliance farmers, restaurateurs and environmentalists work together to foster a farm-to-table program and a sustainable food supply. The alliance also has supported the establishment of local markets and for several years little community markets open only one day a week have popped up all over the county.

Shady Brook Farm is another farm that offers lots of family fun as well as pick-your-own crops. Founded by the Fleming family in Andalusia in 1913, the family gradually moved north finally establishing a new farm near Yardley. While it has a traditional farm market and orchards, it also specializes in what it calls "agritainment" attractions, such as the Hayride of Horror and a Christmas light show, Cruise Nights on Tuesdays, and wine concerts.

Shady Brook also sells plants, trees, shrubs, and gardening supplies. It has a deli, sells dairy products and homemade ice cream, and maintains a kiosk featuring local wines.

The Yerkes family bought None Such Farm in Buckingham in 1926. It is an ancient farm and a previous owner may have named it after Nonsuch Palace in Surrey, built by King Henry VIII and eventually torn down.

None Such Farm today is more classic farm market than it is destination.

The Yerkes family grew sweet corn for the Philadelphia wholesale market for fifty years, but in the 1970s, the corn market changed, forcing the family to switch gears. They built a farm market, limited production, and sold corn locally. They also sell other fresh produce, fresh flowers, farm-raised Black Angus, and operate a deli and a cheese shop.

There are other farms with markets in Bucks County. Some are considered boutique farms and deal with specialty products. They steadfastly breed cattle, unusual sheep, pygmy goats, llamas, alpacas, and buffalos, all of them keeping agriculture alive in a county that flourished on it years ago.

1: A farmer bags gourmet lettuce at the Ottsville Farm Market on Route 611.

2: The Ottsville market is a community market open only on Friday afternoons.

THE CANAL'S SPECIAL APPEAL

On Saturday afternoons in season, polo games bring some excitement to the park.

1: A poodle with corded hair gets some special attention at the annual Bucks County Kennel Club show.

2: Bicyclers are frequently seen riding along the towpath of the Delaware Canal.

3: A lime kiln was once part of the busy nineteenth century village.

Running like a green ribbon along the banks of the Delaware River in Bucks County is the Delaware Canal. Its formal name is the Delaware Division of the Pennsylvania Canal, but it is called simply "the canal" by the thousands of people who live, work, and play nearby.

Today walkers, dog-walkers, joggers, runners, mothers or fathers pushing strollers, bicyclists, hikers, cross-country skiers, and bird watchers use the towpath, and kayaks and canoes glide through the water.

Tinicum County Park runs along the canal. The Tinicum Arts Festival has been held in the park along the canal every July for more than sixty years and the Bucks County Kennel Club has hosted its annual dog show there for seventy years. It's the biggest outdoor dog show in the country.

On Saturday afternoons in the summer, spectators enjoy tailgate picnics as they watch Tinicum Park Polo Club players guide their ponies. It costs only $10 a carload to share the excitement of the sport of kings.

Officially, the canal is now Delaware Canal State Park, and of all the canals dug during the early nineteenth century canal-building era, it is the only one that remains intact, only one mile filled in at its tidewater end. For the most part, it parallels and is in sight of the river; families often picnic near its picturesque camelback bridges.

For about one hundred years after its construction began in 1831, teams of mules, bells jangling on their harnesses, towed ninety-foot-long barges along its length, with boatmen blowing conch shells to alert lock tenders to raise or lower the water level. The canal climbs about 185 feet from south to north.

The barges carried coal from upstate mines and iron to Bristol, where, once out of the canal, barges were roped together and floated downriver to Philadelphia. On return trips, they carried freight.

In 1931, on October 17, the last recorded canal boat traveled the sixty miles north from Bristol to the City of Easton in Northampton County. It was empty, marking the end of a transportation era brought to a halt by railroads. It actually was rescued by Betty Orlemann, a Tinicum mystery novel writer, who organized the Friends of the Delaware Canal, a non-profit group working to protect the historic waterway since 1982.

The canal adds charm to every town and village through which it passes, but perhaps the most intriguing is one in

Tinicum Township, where the canal was built away from the water on a broad river flat stretching from the water to a towering rock palisade. There, hugging the rock is the picturesque village of Uhlerstown, at the site of a covered bridge built in 1832. Constructed of oak, it is 101 feet long and about fifteen feet wide. It is the only one of twelve covered bridges in the county that crosses the canal.

Once called Mexico, the village was renamed in honor of Michael Uhler, a merchant who created a complex little business and industrial center there after his arrival in 1853. Some of the buildings still stand and offer an idea of what life along the canal was like a hundred or so years ago.

Uhler ran a boat-building yard and operated his own fleet of canal boats, ground grain harvested from the surrounding fields in his mill, transported grain and hay to towns along the canal and to the city.

He also operated lime kilns, supplying them with stone cut from quarries north of Easton and delivered on the canal, and built a barn and stables for his mules. The village once included a canal lock, a lock tender's house, a canal boat yard, a hotel, a store and a hay press powered by canal water.

Boatmen and village workers lived in plain little houses nearby. Two larger houses were built of brick, and so were two later buildings.

After canal commerce dried up, the houses were snapped up by artists and city people who used them as studios and summer homes, and a resort flourished there for a while.

Uhlerstown is just one of many villages in sprawling Tinicum, with its ten miles of riverfront. Revolutionary War Colonel Arthur Erwin, an Irishman, who bought the land in 1769, founded another, Erwinna, on the river.

William Penn had intended to establish one of his manors in Tinicum but the plan was never carried out, and the land was sold. He once referred to it as "Indian town."

A mile west of the river in Tinicum and high on a hilltop is Van Sant Airport, one of the last grass airfields on the East Coast and a place where it's easy to think you've stepped back in time. It's one of my favorite places — and apparently a favorite of others, too. They park their cars, walk around, peering into the skies, watching the small aircraft take off and land.

Owned by the county and operated by Sport Aviation Inc., the 200-acre airfield is a busy place when the weather is fair with gliders soaring and vintage biplanes circling high above.

Tinicum Township has some of the most dramatic landscape in Bucks County, with open farm fields, soaring hills, deep woods and creeks that cut through country estates.

It certainly is among the least changed over the years, its roads still following Indian paths along creeks and presenting challenges to motorists — some roads even requiring fording.

The bridge at Uhlerstown is the only one of the county's twelve covered bridges that crosses the canal.

ANCIENT MILLS, MODERN USES

Competition is high for the Phillips Mill art exhibit held annually since 1929.

1: The grounds of the Stover-Myers Mill in Bedminster Township draw picnickers and anglers.

2: The Stover Mill Gallery on River Road is an antique setting for art exhibits on weekends in warmer weather.

3: An old mural on the old Durham gristmill, closed in 1967, was re-painted in 2003.

urviving whole or sometimes only in pieces, old mills are proud remnants of an earlier way of life. Strategically placed on the banks of the Delaware or along creeks during the 1700s and 1800s, they were sturdily built, and the wheels still turned in some until the 1960s. Built mostly of fieldstone, mills have survived where wind and rain often conquered ordinary houses, and they have always been picturesque.

Phillips Mill is a centerpiece of the hamlet that bears its name and lays just a mile-and-a-half north of New Hope on the River Road. Built by Aaron Phillips in 1756, it was owned and operated as a gristmill by four generations of his family. It drew its power from the meandering Primrose Creek.

Now listed on the National Register of Historic Places, the mill has held artistic appeal for more than a century, and according to the register, the hamlet is probably the best preserved of all the mill villages in Bucks County.

The Phillips Mill Community Association, which pays homage annually to local artists, rescued and restored the abandoned mill. Every year since 1929, the association has staged a month-long juried art exhibit there in the fall.

The prestigious show draws a lot of attention in the art world, especially among Manhattan galleries. It includes oils, watercolors, prints, mixed media, drawings and sculptures created by Delaware Valley artists who must live within a 25-mile radius of the mill to submit their work. Attendance is steady and so are sales in the sleepy little village, even during the week, when nearby New Hope is recovering from one weekend of tourists and gearing up for another.

Another old mill that provides an antique setting for art shows is the Stover Mill Gallery on the River Road in Erwinna, Tinicum Township. Built of Pennsylvania fieldstone in 1832 by Henry Stover, it was owned by his descendants for generations. Stover Mill was one of very few mills powered with water drawn directly from the river.

Now headquarters for the Tinicum Civic Association, it has operated as an art gallery since 1959 and is open weekends except in the winter.

The Stover-Myers Mill on twenty-six acres along the Tohickon Creek in Bedminster Township also has great artistic appeal but today it's used mostly for fishing and picnicking. Owned by Jacob Stover in the early 1800s the mill produced flour and animal feed. The mill continued to grind feed and served as an agricultural center until 1955. The county bought it and turned it into a park in 1967.

Another old gristmill is a commanding centerpiece in the Village of Durham. Powered by Cooks Creek, which runs through the village, it was built on the foundation of the ancient iron furnace in 1820.

Later owned by the Riegel family, who added a brick warehouse in 1912, the mill ground flour and feed until 1967. The building is now owned by Durham Township which is raising funds to restore it. A faded and flaking Ceresota flour mural on one wall, much loved by the villagers, was re-painted in 2003.

A MAGNET FOR TOURISTS

Quaint streets and quirky shops draw thousands of tourists
to New Hope on weekends all year long.

1: This shop features collectibles associated with death, but also sells estate jewelry and bird cages.

2: Indian skirts hanging from a railing add a touch of color in early spring.

3: The Parry Mansion along the canal houses a museum.

*P*eople used to say if you sat at a table at the Café de la Paix in Paris, you would eventually see everyone you knew.

Today a table at a café in New Hope might just do the trick. Above all, it's a people-watching town and a go-to place for gay people and others wanting the freedom to express themselves. It's a place where both a restaurant and a police station occupy old churches in feats of architectural recycling.

Tourists roam the pavements, flow through Main Street, and spill over into the alleys of this riverside town. Though little, the town has a big presence. On weekends, they come in cars, boats, canoes, and kayaks; some walk the canal towpath while others ride either bicycles or motorcycles.

New Hope is arty, charming, quirky, and quaint. Its antiques and fine art galleries, arts and craft shops, "different" shops (some quite bizarre), and restaurants tumble over each other on hillside streets and alleys, drawing crowds from all directions and of all ages.

A new Bucks County children's museum opened in 2011 at New Hope's Union Square, will feature interactive exhibits designed to teach children about Bucks County's culture and history.

The town's position on the York Road which crossed both Bucks County and New Jersey's Hunterdon County in the early days of the colonies had a lot to do with its development. Now it's even easier to get to, just a short run from I-95 for day-trippers from New York and Philadelphia and weekenders from all over the world.

The factories that once employed New Hope's residents are long gone, but one has been rebuilt as a shopping and office complex. Another is a luxury condominium complex.

In 2011, the curtain was down at the Bucks County Playhouse, which had been active for seventy years. However, while the darkened theater is no longer the town's centerpiece, a group of investors have breathed new life into the theater.

The colorful nightlife goes on. Bob Egan's New Hope Cabaret Supper Club offers shows that showcase new talent, and almost synonymous with New Hope are the ranks of shining Harleys parked outside Fran's Pub after they blast through town.

Like the other river towns, New Hope was built around a ferry, operating as early as 1722, and a mill named Hope. The mill burned down and after it was rebuilt, the town came to be known as New Hope. Today its main industry is tourism and the townspeople work hard to provide something for everyone — scenic rides through the surrounding countryside on

the New Hope & Ivyland Railroad to its Buckingham Valley station or an outing on an excursion boat operated by Captain Robert Gerenser.

It's fun to walk along the canal towpath where mules once towed barges or visit the 1784 Parry Mansion Museum — or to view the town from mid-river during a walk across the bridge to Lambertville, New Jersey.

Most of all it offers an escape from the humdrum. The fascinating thing about the town is that while it changes, new shops and restaurants falling in place like the pieces of a kaleidoscope, it also remains the same.

Tourists often miss the quiet charm of a residential street.

I have gone to New Hope at least once a year every year since I can remember. My parents took our family there when I was child. I celebrated my twenty-first birthday there with friends — and saw a shooting star.

As a young journalist I often shopped there with friends or by myself during weekdays I had off. I went there on dates, and later with my husband. We took our children to New Hope and now we sometimes leave our empty nest to spend a day there.

For us, and I imagine for most local people, it's a mini-vacation, an escape to another world. The New Hope magic lives on.

Although New Hope is a specific small town, its name often refers to the strip along the Delaware River from Uhlerstown south to Washington Crossing, where the creative and the rich and famous started to buy country homes in the 1920s and 1930s.

Locals looked at them as though they were exotic birds dotting the landscape, and they clustered together in that elongated nest along the river, flying in and out at will. They included playwrights, writers, artists and actors and their "city-folk-in-the-country" antics have been documented in books and on stage and screen.

Bucks County is still a draw for writers and artists but today their homes are scattered. The rough edges of both farmers and sophisticates that created such good comedy have blurred some, and for the most part, the celebrities live more private lives.

Creativity still reigns. The annual New Hope Film Festival draws independent moviemakers from all over the globe.

Interestingly, Bucks County has a century-old motion picture tradition going back to the silent films. *The Perils of Pauline* was filmed on the New Hope & Ivyland Railroad tracks in 1914. More recently, filmmaker M. Night Shyamalan chose Bucks as the site for *Lady in the Water* in 2006; and anyone who saw *Signs*, filmed partly in Bedminster Township in 2002, will never feel the same about a Bucks County cornfield.

The Johnsville Centrifuge and Science Museum now displays the Mercury 7 gondola used during Alan Shepherd's space flight in 1961.

Science as well as art has flourished in Bucks County over the centuries.

A new museum near the place where inventor John Fitch sailed a model of his first steamboat in the 1780s now preserves Space Age history. It's a place where scientists and technologists produced the first heart monitor and the first airplane black box.

The Johnsville Centrifuge and Science Museum in Warminster also is only a dozen or so miles from Growden Mansion in Bensalem, where legend has it that Benjamin Franklin, visiting the estate of his friend, Joseph Galloway, conducted his 1752 kite and key experiment to prove lightning is electricity. At that time, Galloway owned practically all of the land that now is Bensalem.

That experiment today seems like light years away from the opening of the museum in 2011 and from events that took place there during the mid-twentieth century.

On May 5, 2011, the year Warminster was celebrating its 300th anniversary, residents turned out to welcome the *Mercury* 7 gondola used by astronaut Alan Shepard, whose Project Mercury mission exactly fifty years earlier made him the first American in space.

The gondola had been part of the Smithsonian Air and Space Museum collection in Washington, D.C., but had not been on public display for forty-five years. The new museum is situated at the former Naval Air Development Center created in 1947 when the U. S. Navy converted a World War II aircraft factory into laboratories. The Navy conducted experiments in aviation electronics, unmanned aircraft, medicine, jet and rocket engines and armor, and pressure suits worn by the astronauts.

In 1952, the Navy installed the world's largest centrifuge to test the effects of G-forces on a human. Astronauts and pilots trained in the 250-ton centrifuge as part of the Navy's flight program, as did F-14 and X-15 pilots and commercial airline and space shuttle pilots. When it was operating, the centrifuge's motor required enough energy to run 3,000 homes and produced as much

American astronauts and pilots trained on this 250-ton centrifuge at the new museum in Warminster.

as 16,000 horsepower. It simulated the force of gravity.

John Glenn, who orbited Earth in the *Friendship* 7 in 1962, and Neil Armstrong, the first man to walk on the moon, were among thirty-one NASA astronauts in the Mercury, Gemini, and Apollo space programs who trained in the giant centrifuge between 1959 and 1964. A middle school in Fairless Hills is named after Armstrong.

Experiments conducted in the more than thirty laboratories at the 370-acre Johnsville base had a profound affect on everyday life. In addition to heart monitors and black boxes, experiments resulted in transitional lenses, night vision goggles, pilotless drones, crash helmets, ejection seats, and much more.

Interestingly enough, NASA astronaut Daniel W. Bursch, now retired, was born in nearby Bristol in 1957, when the program was still young. He flew four NASA missions, logging 227 days in space beginning in the 1990s.

Astronaut Andrew M. Allen grew up in Richboro — he flew missions on space shuttles *Columbia* and *Atlantis*.

The museum is not far from the Pennsylvania Biotechnology Center of Bucks County in Buckingham. The center, opened in September 2006, is a science/commerce partnership project to foster the development of new life sciences. Members of the partnership search for cures and diagnostic markers of diseases. About thirty companies are working to advance research and regional biotech projects at the center, which was created by the Hepatitis B Foundation and the Institute for Hepatitis and Virus Research. Giant pharmaceutical company Merck & Company turned its entire natural products library over to the researchers in 2011.

The center also offers special training for science students from area colleges.

THE FITCH STEAMBOAT

This is a six-foot-long model of the John Fitch steamboat that operated on the Delaware in the summer of 1790.

Just a year ago while Warminster Township was celebrating its tricentennial, the John Fitch Steamboat Museum opened its doors, calling attention to an event that had occurred 224 years earlier.

The museum, situated on the grounds of Craven Hall, honors the Connecticut Yankee who once lived in Bucks County, and made a successful trial run of his 45-foot steamboat in Philadelphia on Aug. 22, 1787.

While the museum opening was small as such events go, Fitch couldn't have had a more impressive audience at his eighteenth century experimental run. Members of the Constitutional Convention meeting in the city wandered over to the waterfront to watch the trial run, which marked the beginning of a transportation revolution in this country.

Fitch, considered an irascible genius with an uncommon fondness for rum, had designed the steamboat in his Warminster workshop and tested a 23-inch model on a nearby pond.

About 225 years later, a six-foot-long, 100-pound model of the Fitch steamboat constructed by Fred Rosse, a mechanical engineer, was unveiled at the museum's opening ceremonies, and suitably, christened with a mug of rum. Museum officials tested the model on a Warminster pond, just as Fitch had done.

The museum is maintained by the Craven Hall Historical Society and is based in a former carriage house on the grounds of the restored 1840s Greek Revival manor house.

The museum was created because the folks at the society wanted to honor Fitch, whose steamboat cut

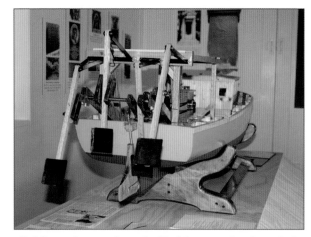

Paddles at the stern kept the Fitch boat moving through the water long before Robert Fulton designed his steamboat.

through the water two decades before that of Robert Fulton, the man commonly credited with its invention. In fact, Fitch won the innovation battle, but Fulton had extensive financial backing and his venture was a commercial success. So it's his name the country associates with the first steamboat, but in Bucks County, it's all about John Fitch.

With the economy still sagging after the Revolutionary War, Fitch had problems raising funds, but he plugged away on an even newer, improved design, and that steamship provided the first commercial steamboat service. In the summer of 1790 Fitch's sixty-foot steamboat, *Perseverance*, ran a regular schedule on the Delaware between Philadelphia, Bristol and Trenton, New Jersey. It wasn't until August 7, 1807,

that Fulton's steamboat, *Clermont*, traveled the Hudson River from New York City to Albany.

The *Perseverance* carried twenty-five partying passengers who munched on sausages and drank beer and rum. The ship traveled 3,000 miles in all, but it lost money on every voyage, and Fitch's investors vanished.

An embittered Fitch moved to Kentucky where just before drinking himself to death, he correctly predicted, "The day will come when some more powerful man will get fame and riches from my invention."

Even so, Bucks County did not forget Fitch, and newer steamboats called at Bucks County's riverside towns for more than 125 years after the inventor launched that first commercial passenger service.

Even before Fitch, shipbuilders had gathered along the banks of the Delaware in the area of Philadelphia and especially in Bristol where the industry accounted for much of the town's prosperity in the early years of the nineteenth century.

Shipyards lined the river and the banks of Mill Creek in Bristol; the schooner *Morning Star*, supposedly one of the best on the seas, was built there by a prominent ship builder named John Reed.

Shipbuilding continued as an important industry in Bristol. In 1917, W. Averell Harriman, who later became ambassador to the Soviet Union during the Cold War, bought one of the shipyards. He named the yard Merchant Shipbuilding. The Emergency Fleet Corporation joined it and built twelve shipways, turning out forty cargo ships between 1918 and 1921.

The 100-year-old Moravian Pottery and Tile Works is a working history museum.

Step through the antique wooden door with its wrought iron hinges and into the Moravian Pottery and Tile Works and you'll feel as though you've walked right into the Middle Ages even though the business is marking its 100th anniversary this year.

For the most part, this ancient shop is dark and caught up in the atmosphere of yesteryear — and that's what's totally mesmerizing about it. It's truly wondrous that the decorative Mercer tiles with their exploding colors and often wildly imaginative designs spring from what appears to be a mysterious womb-like place. That they do so is the craft, and the joy, of today's artisans who turn blocks of local clay into handmade tiles using methods perfected one hundred years ago.

The pottery and tile works is maintained as a working history museum and operated by Bucks County's Department of Parks and Recreation. Built in a U-shaped configuration, its arcade walls opening on a broad courtyard, it looks like an ancient cloister set in the spacious lawn at the east end of the Mercer Mile in Doylestown, the county seat.

The Mercer Mile's other attractions, Mercer Museum and Fonthill are owned by the Bucks County Historical Society; the three buildings form a National Historic Landmark District. All three structures were built of reinforced concrete by Renaissance man Henry Chapman Mercer, Doylestown's favorite son.

Mercer built the tile works during the Arts and Crafts movement, a kind of anti-machine trend that brought new attention to, and respect for, handmade articles after the Industrial Revolution.

Mercer constructed the museum that bears his name to house his huge collection of Early American artifacts and tools. Fonthill is his castle-like home with tiles lining walls and ceilings and narrow passageways and peeking around corners. Tiles also are embedded in both exterior and interior walls of the tile works.

It took two years for Mercer and a handful of workers to build the tile works. Workers completed it in 1912, replacing an old pottery Mercer had hoped to bring to life. While the pottery venture did not succeed, his subsequent tile making had a spectacular result. Mercer personally directed the work there until his death in 1930.

Original Mercer tiles can be found in many fine old homes in Doylestown and in schools and colleges, libraries and other public buildings throughout Pennsylvania, including the floors at the state capitol building in Harrisburg. In 1904, Mercer won the St. Louis Exposition grand prize for his unusual fireplace, wall and floor tiles.

Mercer tiles also were sold extensively throughout the United States and abroad. Two of the more surprising places they appear are at Grauman's Chinese Theater in Hollywood and the Casino in Monte Carlo.

Today, the tile workers, all of whom are trained artists, follow Mercer's process to create the handmade tiles using his original plaster molds, many of them based on folk art designs copied from old Moravian cast-iron stove plates. As many as 40,000 visitors each year watch the artisans making the tiles and stamping them with the distinctive MOR mark and the date. No two tiles are identical.

Old mosaic tiles add a touch of color to the rough concrete walls of the tile works.

A modern wing houses a gallery and will be used to host events at the Mercer Museum in Doylestown.

MERCER MUSEUM
AND LIBRARY

The exterior of the Mercer Museum is an impressive landmark.

Doylestown's two landmark museums — the Mercer and the Michener — named after the town's favorite sons are perfect examples of old places with new faces. In 2011, both museums added new wings.

Now a world-class showplace, the Mercer Museum was completed in 1916 by Doylestown historian/archaeologist/collector Henry Chapman Mercer to house his 50,000-piece collection of pre-Industrial Revolution tools and artifacts.

Mercer was one of the founders of the Bucks County Historical Society and when he died in 1930, he left his "concrete castle" to a trust. It remained fairly untouched until the 1970s when the society took over its administration, added a professional staff and improved and expanded the building which also houses the Spruance Library, a research facility specializing in Bucks County history and culture.

Now, a new $12.5 million wing, opened last June, provides an additional 13,000-square-feet of space, letting visitors see many items that show how earlier Americans lived and worked.

Mercer and a small crew of workers built the towering structure of concrete reinforced with iron rods.

The six-level museum, topped with roof galleries is built around a central court with alcoves displaying the tools of Early American trades such as butter and cheese making, cider making, glass blowing, tin smithing, leather working, and coopering.

The boxy new wing standing at its base is also constructed of concrete, its simplicity complementing the turrets and many-windowed walls of the original building. The side of the wing facing the castle is all windows and skylights showing off the old structure.

Although the new gallery at the Mercer Museum is impressive, the real attention-grabber for the visitor — and there are about 80,000 a year — is the original central court. Hanging from its rafters high above are a Conestoga wagon, a whaleboat and the gallows from the old county prison.

Every time I go to the museum I see myself as a child staring horrified at the gallows when I first saw it, but I also remember running round and round the alcoves that still hold the tools of more than sixty Early American trades.

The shining instruments in the little surgery and the dentist's office terrified me, too, but I liked the printer's shop. I guess my dreams of a becoming a writer were already taking form in my five-year-old head, because I was particularly taken with Edgar Allan Poe's pen and ink well. I ran to see that every time I went to the museum. It's still there.

The energy-efficient project includes a "green" roof, a rain garden, recycled wall paneling, water-conserving features and permeable paving in the parking lot.

One of this years' exhibits is "The Apron Collection: A Patchwork of American Recollections," including photographs and 155 vintage aprons telling their stories. Next year an exhibit will center on the Civil War and the Bucks County/Delaware Valley home front.

The second and newer museum, the James A. Michener Art Museum, which opened in 1988, occupies the remnants of the abandoned Bucks County Prison. Michener, a Doylestown native, had an extensive art collection.

It's an imposing presence with twenty-three foot high walls that separated a century's worth of prisoners from society, allowing them to consider their crimes and repent in isolation.

The old sally port gate no longer slams shut when visitors enter the walled yard. They find there a garden, filled with sculpture, and frequently, in the summer, children taking art classes. An Isaac Witkin bronze sculpture, Waif's Anchors, stands at the spot where hangings once took place — the last in 1914.

The museum itself occupies what was once the warden's house. Built in 1885, the compound closed exactly a hundred years later.

Now the Michener is adding a new wing, the Edgar N. Putman Event Center, a 2,700-square-foot space for concerts, lectures, exhibition openings, weddings and other private parties.

The light-filled, all-glass structure with a solid roof will extend into the sculpture garden, and sliding doors will allow passage into the outdoors. Guests will also be able to enter the galleries.

The museum showcases the works of important regional artists and plays host to special touring exhibitions. An international exhibit this year is an April through August display of a collection of religious paintings from the Uffizi Gallery in Florence called "Offering of the Angels."

1: The James A. Michener Art Museum is housed in the former Bucks County Prison.

2: In the museum's courtyard a modern sculpture is centered on the spot where the gallows once stood.

SEARCHING
FOR THE SOUL

The arts building is one of nineteen scattered across the
Nakashima complex. *Courtesy of Nakashima Studios.*

Sunlight pours through the glass wall of Nakashima's conoid studio in Solebury. *Courtesy of Nakashima Studios.*

The hillside conoid studio, surrounded by trees, faces south. *Courtesy of Nakashima Studios.*

The Nakashima compound was placed on the National Register of Historic Places in 2010. Master craftsmen who follow the artisan's principles under the direction of his daughter carry on his work.

Today, Nakashima's work can be seen in prestigious museum collections, private homes and public places all over the world. The Nakashima Reading Room at the James A. Michener Reading Room in Doylestown is an oasis of peace and beauty designed by the woodworker's daughter and featuring furnishings made by her father's craftsmen.

I recall the first time my parents drove past Nakashima's studio. I was little more than a child, but I was fascinated with the roof-line, which reminded me of a seashell. I grew up following Nakashima's career and admiring his wonderful furniture.

I remember, too, many years later, how surprised and pleased I was to stumble upon one of his peace altars. My husband and I were in Manhattan to attend my Barnard College class reunion. We strolled across Broadway to the Columbia University campus. The door to St. Paul's Chapel was open and we wandered in. There, in the south transept, was this incredible piece of polished oak — another Nakashima peace altar. I knew he had done a lot of work for Columbia; I learned later that though this altar was made after his death, it was based on his designs and materials. It commemorates Columbia's war dead from twentieth century conflicts.

It is inspiring that this artisan, who, with his family, was a victim of war and injustice, was driven to celebrate peace in such a beautiful way. I don't think there's any doubt that William Penn would have approved.

*B*ucks County has been famous for years for its many excellent artisans, but it is likely the name of the late George Nakashima, architect turned woodworker and furniture designer, will long be paramount among them. Cast off by the United States government he nevertheless brought his love of nature and his skills to Bucks County in 1943 and his new neighbors embraced him.

The woodworker, who lived in Solebury for half a century, always searched for the soul of the tree, celebrating the unique natural features as he turned its wood into elegant, functional pieces.

It is fitting that he now lies buried in the Thompson Memorial Cemetery across the road from the Columbus Oak, a gigantic umbrella of a tree said to have been alive when Columbus sailed to the New World.

Nakashima and his daughter, Mira Nakashima-Yarnall, also an architect, who now is creative director at the shop her father founded in 1943, loved that tree. A cross made from its branches marks his grave.

It is fitting also that this man who was persecuted by his adopted country chose to live here in Penn's home county.

George Nakashima, who had grown up in Spokane, Washington, was among the thousands of Japanese-Americans placed in internment camps during World War II by a fearful wartime administration.

While detained behind barbed wire in Idaho with his wife and infant daughter, Nakashima learned woodworking from a Japanese carpenter. After the family's release, they moved to a Solebury chicken farm, where the woodworker later opened a hillside shop and a studio.

Nakashima designed and constructed that first building of wood and local fieldstone, capping it with a shell-like roof. Over the years, he added eighteen buildings to accommodate his growing business.

Among his most beautiful public works is a series of Peace Altars. The first, made of matched boards from a black walnut tree, was installed at the Episcopal Cathedral of St. John the Divine in New York City. It was dedicated New Year's Eve 1986 with a concert conducted by Leonard Bernstein.

TODAY'S LENAPE VILLAGE

Two wigwams placed together create a longhouse at Churchville Nature Center's Lenape Village.

1: A volunteer demonstrates the way the Lenapes, using a stick and string, started a fire.

2: Schoolchildren take turns touching a bearskin at the village.

So much of Bucks County's past is attached to the Lenni Lenapes. Today, those intrigued with the people who lived here before we did can see how the natives lived.

Lenape Village, a hands-on living history exhibit in Upper Southampton Township, offers a first-hand experience of what it was like to live on the banks of the Neshaminy Creek, existing through all seasons and thriving from the bounty nature provided.

It's a scene from another century. A long, narrow Indian trail leads from the road to a clearing in the woods where wigwams are set in a lush meadow close to a creek. Animal hides are draped across a rope looking, at first glance, almost like laundry, corn and squash are set out to dry. The thunder of a drum begins.

Buckskin-clad volunteers playing the roles of the original people, the Lenni Lenapes, appear. A young brave shows how the sparks from friction can start a fire, a squaw works with flying fingers turning the strands of natural fibers into strong cords. A man works on the hides, a woman prepares clay to make pottery, another, her dark hair in a long braid, tends to the cooking while still another works among the neat garden rows. The Indians, an environmentalist's dream people, more or less recycled everything, wasting nothing.

The Lenape Village is an echo of what probably happened here just before the white man arrived. Indian villages covered the county then, especially along the Delaware River and its tributaries. Streams were the Lenapes' natural boundaries, while the white man tended to run his borders along hills or mountain ridges.

The Bucks County Department of Parks and Recreation operates the village, which is part of the Churchville Nature Center. Busloads of schoolchildren from several states are delivered daily to the village throughout the season.

One of the first known Indian villages discovered by settlers was situated on Biles Island in the Delaware River about a mile south of Falls of the Delaware, present-day Morrisville. The falls actually were and still are a series of rapids that defy navigation, and an important meeting place.

In fact, the deed given to William Penn by the Lenapes, the first of the Indian grants to him, was signed July 15, 1682, at the Falls.

Early maps show Indian fields and villages in many townships. The sites, plowed over now, didn't all survive but many Lenape names took root in towns and streams throughout the county. They run through the alphabet: Aquetong, Buckwampum, Cuttalossa, Holicong, Lahaska, Neshaminy, Nockamixon, Paunacussing, Perkasie, Tinicum, Tohickon, Towhee and more.

A volunteer at the Lenape Village tells schoolchildren how the Indians prepared animal pelts.

Several prominent villages were situated in Buckingham and Solebury in 1690 and an Indian village once occupied what is now Washington Crossing State Park. Indian mounds and what may have been an ancient crematory were found in Durham, and sacred sites are found throughout the county. Scholars believe the Lenapes worshipped among the gigantic rocks at Manderfield, a private preserve in West Rockhill Township, and at the rocky top of Haycock Mountain.

The Lenapes used jasper to make their arrow and spear points, and an important jasper quarry and Indian remains were found on Durham's Rattlesnake Hill.

Three ancient village sites were established just north of The Narrows and evidence shows both Shawnees and Delawares camped there. Perhaps occupants worked at the nearby jasper mines.

One of the villages was situated at the mouth of Durham Cave, an enormous cave with several chambers. Once a huge attraction, the cave was ruined as a result of too much tourist traffic and unrestrained souvenir-taking. In 1893, Doylestown archaeologist Henry Mercer camped in a tent nearby spending a month with workers as they unearthed ancient relics.

The Lenapes are believed to have traveled from the west before Europeans arrived. They're considered Woodlands Indians from the Late Woodland period, which ran from 1000 to 400 years ago.

But the earliest known occupation of this area was 16,000 years ago, and evidence of prehistoric man is abundant along the Delaware, especially in the areas of Riegelsville and Durham.

In 1892, Charles Laubach of Durham read a paper called "Prehistoric Man" before members of the Bucks County Historical Society detailing his findings of an ancient hearth as well as argillite, quartz and jasper spear points, arrow heads and net sinkers in a drift of stones he believed was deposited by glaciers along the Delaware.

Seventeen years later he gave his personal collection of 1,500 artifacts to the Museum of the University of Pennsylvania.

Huge rocks such as these in West Rockhill Township often marked Lenape sacred sites, which are found all over the county.

GENERATIONS ON THE FARM

The Trauger-Kressman farmhouse, built in 1779, has been occupied by the Trauger family ever since.

It's an unmistakable Upper Bucks landmark — eighteenth century stone farmhouse, barn and outbuildings, fields plowed straight and rich with greenery. Adding to the charm is an old stone washhouse where boiling wash water heated the bake oven behind it.

It is unique. Eight generations of the same family have farmed it and members of the ninth are working the soil with their toy John Deere tractors.

The sixty-acre Trauger-Kressman farm in Durham Township is both icon of the past and an enduring and successful venture in a time when many small farms have fallen victim to competition from giant agri-businesses.

Tucked between the Delaware River and the Delaware Canal, which runs along Route 611 at that point, the property is now owned by the family's seventh generation and is as close to the idealized nostalgic vision of a farm as one can get.

It is a working, prosperous vegetable farm with a busy roadside market and a reputation for outstanding strawberries and corn. Crops include other berries and vegetables. Now, boutique vegetables hold a special appeal for the many New Yorkers who have weekend homes in the nearby hills.

Manhattan is only about eighty miles from Durham Township and many city folk stop at Traugers to stock their summer kitchens. In June Traugers' strawberries glow like gems against the lush green leaves and the fields are populated with customers kneeling along the rows selecting their own fruit. When the Concorde flew between New York and Paris, those picking in the field would hear its sonic boom.

During October's Pumpkin Festival, bright pumpkins line the lawn, and children ride along a dusty lane in an antique farm wagon pulled by Belgian draught horses.

Agricultural experts have claimed the farm has the best soil in Bucks County. Farmer Myron Kressman and his wife, LeeAnn Trauger Kressman, rise with the birds and often work straight through until bedtime. It is hard, often monotonous and never-ending work. Myron, who studied agriculture and business at The Pennsylvania State University, also worked for the legendary Burpee Seed Co. in Doylestown and for a nearby farm bureau. When the appeal of the outdoors overcame him, he turned to farming with Fred Trauger, LeeAnn's father. Myron gradually introduced new farming practices and new crops.

The Kressmans live in the handsome old farmhouse along the canal where LeeAnn's parents lived until their deaths. Built of fieldstone, the front portion bears a 1779 date stone and was built by William Abbot as a hotel called the Half Moon and Seven Stars.

1: The small stone wash house by the canal has a bake oven attached to the back.

2: People travel for miles to buy Trauger strawberries in June; in July, sweet corn is the biggest attraction.

3: Belgian draught horses pull wagonloads of children for tours of the farm.

Pumpkins carpet the lawn at the farmhouse in October.

The sign, typical of the times, bore only the symbols and no words. Many colonial travelers either did not speak English or were illiterate.

The Half Moon and Seven Stars apparently was a popular name for inns, cropping up in England after the Crusades and possibly having had either religious or navigational significance. At any rate, the sign survives and is now part of the Mercer Museum's collection of old tavern signs.

The rear portion of the house was added in 1841 and the hotel operated until 1852. The canal, built during the 1830s, cut through the property and LeeAnn said she had been told workers would sneak into the barn and steal hams left hanging from the rafters to cure.

The farmer's daughters have their own boutique businesses on the property. Laura Helfrich grows flowers and is in charge of the greenhouse and Rachael Roney, who is a baker, sells pies and other goodies in the farm store, and makes and decorates wedding cakes. Laura, her husband and ninth-generation sons, Clayton and Landon, live in a newer home on the property.

A Lisa Naples ceramic crow stands guard at the garden fence.

New Hope is where Bucks County's passion for art first sparked, but now the entire county is afire with the arts with community groups serving as incubators in Langhorne, Perkasie, Sellersville, and Quakertown.

While the quaint riverside town gave its name to the New Hope School of Artists, it is the tiny village of Phillips Mill a stone's throw north of New Hope that was the first home of the artists now known as the Pennsylvania Impressionists.

Painter William Langston Lathrop moved to Phillips Mill from New York City in 1899. One of the founders of what was to become the world-famous New Hope art colony, he painted, taught and entertained at his home and studio where he and his wife conducted a salon.

Besides Lathrop, artists included Daniel Garber, Edward Redfield, John Folinsbee, Walter Schofield, Fern Coppedge, Walter Emerson Baum, and Clarence Johnson. The New Hope group exhibited together in the United States and Europe between 1916 and 1918.

Baum, the only one of the Impressionists born in Bucks County, spread his influence to the neighboring Lehigh Valley. He founded both the Baum School of Fine Art in Allentown and the Allentown Art Museum.

The other members of the colony, mostly from New York and Philadelphia and drawn by Bucks' natural beauty, put riverside villages and their surrounding fields on the map. Their handsome and now treasured landscapes laid the fine arts foundation throughout the entire region and created a hunger for local landscapes that still gnaws at many Bucks artists, both professional and amateur.

The James A. Michener Art Museum in Doylestown lists a database of more than 350 professional artists, dead and alive, with ties to the county. More than two hundred of those are painters and illustrators; the rest include sculptors, photographers, composers, musicians, videographers, and writers — and some writers who paint and some painters who write.

Included are master craftsmen who have national reputations, such as woodworker Robert Whitley of Solebury who designs and makes furniture. Whitley, who has a national reputation, made a chess set presented by President Richard Nixon to the Soviet Union that is now in The Hermitage in St. Petersburg. He also copied President John F. Kennedy's Oval Office desk for the Kennedy Memorial Library in Boston.

A young craftsman whose studio is far from New Hope is Bil Mitchell, who is still building his reputation. In his Guitar Parlor in Riegelsville, he designs and creates customized acoustic guitars that sell for thousands of dollars.

Artist Scott Hanna inks in the dark shadows for Spiderman comics and his wife, Pamela Ptak, designs women's apparel using haute couture artistry. They have separate studios in their Durham Township home.

Kate White, longtime editor-in-chief of *Cosmopolitan*, splits her time between Durham and Manhattan and writes the Bailey Weggins mystery novels as well as thrillers.

There are many, many more artists and writers in residence in Bucks County.

Galleries, studios, and shops all over the county overflow with works of art all year long. Artists set their easels up along country roads in all seasons; hardly a barn or pasture or creek has escaped notice of the artist's searching eye.

Many contemporary artists hold art degrees from impressive academies and have earned national reputations. In addition, amateur artists have sprung from every part of the county, and individual community art groups thrive. Some artists are natives, but many have been drawn by the area's artistic reputation and its ready market.

Lisa Naples, a native Bucks Countian and a ceramic artist who lives and works in Doylestown,

1: Luthier Bil Mitchell builds an acoustic guitar at his Guitar Parlor shop in Riegelsville.

2: Deborah Bruns-Thomas works with the stained paper of used teabags to add color and transparency to her creations.

says, "The Impressionists were contemporary in their day, but they are no longer creating."

Naples and other contemporary artists, painters, photographers, and woodworkers took part in a springtime tour conducted from 2008 through 2011 that allowed the community to visit Bucks County artists in their studios. "These are living, breathing people who are creating art every day," Naples says.

While nature initially led to art in Bucks County and is still a leading subject, in an unexpected twist, art has led to the nurturing of the environment in what is considered the watershed of picturesque Gallows Run.

Artist Todd Stone, who paints at his farm in Nockamixon Township, also has a studio in Manhattan's Tribeca, where he watched from his window the 2001 terrorist attacks on the World Trade Center. He painted his anguish on that horrendous day in a series of watercolors entitled "Witness."

Later, he sought solace at his farm only to find developers carving up the neighboring fields. Horrified, he formed the Gallows Run Watershed Association, gathering a group of volunteers to help save the land.

The non-profit group managed to reduce the number of houses built and continues to map water supply and drainage along Gallows Run. Each year members stage an Art for Conservation event, displaying the work of local artists to benefit land conservation and environmental education.

THE UNDERGROUND RAILROAD

While it's generally known in Bucks County that Quakers and non-Quakers who were abolitionists helped runaway slaves to escape to the North, there is no paper trail documenting it, partly due to its secrecy and danger.

But now a handsome bronze statue in Bristol Lions Park honors Harriet Tubman, the abolitionist slave who repeatedly made dangerous Underground Railroad trips to rescue more than three hundred fellow slaves from western Maryland.

Now that statue shouts loud and clear that Bristol played an important role in the Underground Railroad, and, several families in town can trace their ancestry to the Tubman family.

The railroad was merely a code word for a secret network of places or "stations" provided by those opposed to slavery. Those who guided slaves and provided shelter were called "conductors."

The slaves traveled in secret by night following the North Star, and those going to the northern states nearly always passed through Pennsylvania. Heading north from Philadelphia, some would hug the banks of the Delaware River or travel by boat. A number of homeowners near the river in Bristol took in slaves and then passed them on to stations in other riverside towns before they crossed into New Jersey heading for New York and/or Canada.

The operation was quite sophisticated and was set up on a kind of "need to know" basis, with conductors given only a limited knowledge of the escape route. Quakers and many churches were part of the operation. The slaves followed a route that was informal, often impromptu and likely to zigzag to confuse any following slave-catchers.

One place definitely known to be a station was the Continental Hotel along the canal in Yardley. It's still there and is now called the Continental Tavern.

Just as Southern abolitionists had helped some brave slaves escape, there were those in the North who favored slavery and would report this illegal transport of slaves to the authorities, collecting pay for their information. Absolute secrecy was essential; it was a dangerous enterprise for slaves as well as conductors.

There's still a lot of secrecy surrounding the Underground Railroad — and a lot of legend to run through to reach reality. For example, I grew up knowing about secret rooms in basements in Bristol only to discover that some never existed, but others did.

When I was a child I was told by a person who claimed first-hand knowledge a secret room existed in the Keene Mansion on the river; however, when the mansion was eventually torn down, none was found.

My grandmother, Mary Wheeler Gorman, worked as a housekeeper before her marriage in a house built by John Reed, an orphan who, like Moses, was found in a bundle of reeds and given that appropriate name by his adoptive parents.

My research shows that house had a hiding place for slaves. My grandmother, of course, worked there long after the Underground Railroad had succeeded in its mission. She must have known about it, but she never told me. Grandmothers, like old houses, do keep secrets.

A waterfront statue of Harriet Tubman honors the woman who helped slaves escape to Underground Railroad stations.

A Bensalem farmer, Robert Purvis, was the son of a wealthy white English cotton broker and a freeborn black woman from Charleston, South Carolina. An ardent abolitionist, he used his Bensalem home as a station for runaway slaves. In one instance, he had hired an escaped black and helped find jobs for the man's brothers. When slave-catchers arrived to take the slave back to Maryland, Purvis fought valiantly for the man's freedom, even to the point of hiring a lawyer to defend him. The trial was dismissed by a sympathetic judge, and Purvis took the slave to a safe haven. Purvis later helped William Lloyd Garrison organize the American Anti-Slavery Society and served as its first president.

Many historians have written about the Underground Railroad activity in the eastern part of Bucks County but have ignored what happened in Quakertown at the time. It's just as interesting.

Quaker Richard Moore was a schoolmaster who later became a successful potter, and in 1833, built a mansion about two blocks from Richland Meeting.

He cared about the runaways and his home became an Underground Railroad station, actually the most important one in Upper Bucks, for thirty years.

He sent the slaves, some of whom had traveled up through neighboring Montgomery County, off to his pottery where they were hidden in delivery wagons, taken north to Milford Township, where they moved on to the Moravians in Bethlehem and from there to New York.

Moore was one conductor who kept written records and by the end of the Civil War, the list of slaves he had helped had grown to six hundred.

This old Yardley hotel had a secret room to hide slaves traveling the Underground Railroad to the North. They were hidden in at least one other Yardley home.

Bucks County's third courthouse becomes an administration center when a new courthouse is completed.

oylestown, like a monarch overseeing a kingdom from a raised throne, is set on a hill where it can see and be seen. It definitely makes a strong statement.

It is the seat of government in Bucks County, where license is given and justice dispensed, where the powerful and the poor appear when called.

Centrally situated, it has been the county seat since 1813, and the town with its substantial homes literally breathes permanency.

With several exceptions Doylestown today is a nineteenth century town surrounded by acres of housing developments still "new" by town standards; however, in the early 1700s, while history was happening south and north of it, it was little more than an outpost in the wilderness.

Since its designation as the county seat, three courthouses have been built: the first in 1813, the second in 1878, and the present one in 1962. Even more imposing, the fourth is on its way.

The current courthouse will be turned into an administrative building when a new eight-story Justice Center is completed in 2013 with an expected price tag of $84 million. The new center is being constructed on the site of the county's parking garage just across Main Street from the current courthouse — still on the hill.

Even as change has come slowly to Doylestown, it has raced through the county in the last fifty years. The new courthouse is required to handle the increased workload created with the population explosion; nevertheless, its construction and projected appearance have met with controversy. History shows each successive courthouse faced similar outrage.

Lawyers' Row with its Federal style buildings stretches along East Court Street directly across from the round courthouse built in 1962.

Its lampposts hung with flowers, Doylestown virtually blooms with money and elegant shops, interesting restaurants and historic pride, a proper, wealthy matron of a town expecting newcomers to pay their dues.

Women have always been a force in the community. The Village Improvement Association, organized in 1895 by fourteen women, is the only women's club in the country to own a community hospital. Doylestown Hospital, founded in a single house by the group in 1923 and now a regional health center, has a staff of more than 420 physicians with about forty specialties.

The VIA also owns the James-Lorah House, a seventeen-room house-museum built in 1844 on North Main Street, and has added an auditorium complex for community use.

A bit removed from town is the English Tudor mansion named Aldie built in 1927 by the Mercer family.

Doylestown today is a lawyer's town and attorneys' offices occupy many of the beautiful old homes. Lawyers Row on East Court Street is stacked with tall Federal Era buildings erected in the mid 1830s. One was the brick home of historian W.W.H. Davis, now the offices of 135-year-old Eastburn & Gray, Doylestown's largest law firm.

Public buildings, mansions, cottages, carriage houses showing so many styles and combinations of styles throughout town are an architect's dream. Nearly 1,200 buildings comprise the town's historic district.

The intersection of State and Main streets is crowned with the handsome brick Lenape Hall, built in 1874 and once the site of an outdoor farmer's market, and the fieldstone Fountain House Hotel, built around 1756, and now housing a Starbucks Coffee shop.

My favorite place in town still is the tall, narrow Intelligencer Building erected in 1876. I worked for the Intelligencer for fifteen years in a newer office on Broad Street.

My colleague, the late Lester Trauch, reporter and Doylestown legend, had worked at the old 10 East Court Street building, and I was told he occasionally leaned out the upstairs newsroom window and shouted (in a stentorian voice) to friends on the street.

I liked the idea of working for a newspaper that was so old. First published in 1804, it was a weekly called the *Pennsylvania Correspondent and Farmers' Advertiser*. Its first publisher was a man named Asher Miner and it flourished under various publishers and names until the word Intelligencer found its way into the title in 1827—and it's still there.

It still amazes me that the paper was printed in the basement of the old building until 1973. The two dailies, *The Intelligencer* and the larger *Bucks County Courier Times*, based in Levittown, owned by Calkins Media Inc., are now printed and distributed from a giant complex in Falls Township.

It is believed the town is named after the original Doyle's Tavern, which was licensed in 1745, and situated where the Fountain House now stands. The land was originally owned by the Free Society of Traders of London.

The Bucks County Historical Society conducts walking tours through the shaded streets. Tours also are scheduled at the heavily treed Doylestown Cemetery, final resting place of the many illustrious people who once walked these streets.

Sometimes it seems as though the town itself is eclipsed by interest in the Mercer Mile, but that tourist magnet does bring visitors to town and they "discover" Doylestown and its many shops and restaurants.

1: Anthropologist Margaret Mead grew up in this blue Victorian and graduated from Doylestown High School before going on to Barnard College.

2: The Intelligencer building, erected in 1876 with a mixture of architectural styles, housed a working newspaper and press until 1973.

THAT VILLAGE CHARM

This stone building in the village of Solebury houses the post office.

In Bucks County, villages are as hard to define as they are charming. Founded in different centuries for varying reasons, or for little or no reason at all, they seemed to just spring from the soil at irregular intervals.

Some have disappeared leaving little more than a name as a neighborhood while others still exist in a "don't blink or you'll miss it" state.

Some grew up around old taverns or mills on colonial crossroads. Some came to life as workers settled around a rural industry, such as a tanning yard or a quarry. Some bore names such as Elephant, Finland, Jericho and Mozart.

Carversville, listed on the National Register of Historic Places, is a particularly charming little village in Solebury Township. Once called Indian Village, it was first surveyed in 1702. It became prosperous with the establishment of several mills and a hat factory along the Paunacussing Creek.

A prime example of a nineteenth century farm village, it is centered on a village square. A place where small shops once flourished, the square now houses an inn and a general store that once was a stable. It is a wealthy village with an array of handsomely restored Victorian homes lining its narrow roads.

Since 1871, the Carversville Christian Church has sponsored its annual oyster-pork dinner in October. Church members now prepare more than eight hundred meals, using oysters flown from California and local produce, and civic groups pitch in to help with traffic and parking. A lot has changed in more than 140 years, but the tradition lives on.

1: The Carversville Inn is the focal point of the Village Square in the town that was once called Indian Town.

2: Founded in 1740, the Black Bass Inn was a stronghold for Tories before the Revolutionary War.

Kintnersville, the village closest to my home, was named after the German-born Kintner/Gunter family, which yielded several military men: Richard, who enlisted in the Continental Army at age thirteen; Colonel Jacob Kintner, who was Bucks County sheriff in the 1820s; and Major Hugh Kintner, Bucks recorder of deeds in the 1850s.

The village itself is situated in the valley of Gallows Run at the northern end of the River Road, now called the Delaware River Scenic Drive. Its population has hovered around seventy for years. In the mid-nineteenth century, it was a thriving lumber town, its few Victorian houses built of red brick carried to town aboard canal boats.

A gristmill turned antique shop and a post office are the village center. A person can live in one of four townships — Durham, Haycock, Nockamixon, or Springfield — and still have a Kintnersville postal address, offering as much confusion as possible for visitors and deliverymen.

Lumberville, a riverside village in Solebury Township, has survived flood after flood. It is the home of the Black Bass Hotel, built in 1740, and according to legend, it denied lodging to George Washington because the owner was a Loyalist.

Perhaps, perhaps not, but a former owner, the late Herbert Ward, was a confirmed Anglophile and the Duke and Duchess of Windsor were once Ward's guests there as they made their peripatetic way around the world after his abdication as King Edward VIII. The hotel, closed for a while, was extensively renovated in 2009.

Fern Coppedge, the only woman among the Pennsylvania Impressionists — and my personal favorite, for her vibrant colors and saucy landscapes — lived in Lumberville.

Lumberville is inextricably tied to Tinsman Bros. Inc., a lumber yard and hardware store that's been in business since 1785. The oldest lumberyard in the country, it has survived for 227 years despite often devastating flooding of the Delaware River.

The village of Center Bridge sees a lot of traffic. It's home of the Center Bridge Inn as well as Dilly's Corner, an iconic little drive-in, where a clerk passes out a playing card when you place your order at a window and calls the card when the food is ready to be picked up.

In contrast to most of the villages which grew with the centuries and often show various architectural styles, Dyerstown, a few miles north of Doylestown seems trapped in one era.

Dyerstown was known to be there in 1763 and it stopped in its tracks in 1870, retaining its original appearance. A stone mill and eight stone houses built

together along the road all belonged to members of the Dyer family. The village was bypassed when Route 611 was built and the tiny town with its narrow road never was updated. The Dyers opposed development and the town remains a lasting image of village life as it was.

Bucks County also has two lost villages, both at bottoms of lakes. One is a tiny nineteenth century lead mining center now under Peace Valley Park's Lake Galena, created as a county flood-control measure in 1972.

Submerged in the waters of Lake Nockamixon is an entire farming community. The state condemned 290 properties in the 1960s to form the state park. Residents of the Tohickon Valley were forced to re-locate and a road was moved so the 1,450-acre lake could be created. Lost in the process were pre-Revolutionary stone houses, barns, mills and old iron bridges. The lake, designed for recreation for residents of Bucks, Philadelphia, and the Lehigh Valley was completed in the 1970s.

Dilly's Corner in Centre Bridge, a hamburger haven in an area full of elegant restaurants, is always busy in the warmer months.

IT'S STILL CURTAIN TIME

The Bucks County Playhouse is an imposing feature of New Hope's landscape.

*T*he footlights still shine at the embattled old Bucks County Playhouse, New Hope's famous centerpiece.

Threatened with extinction in 2010 and darkened throughout 2011, it has been rescued by Jed Bernstein, a Broadway producer; Kevin and Sherri Daugherty, whose family-owned Bridge Street Foundation provided funding; and Peggy McRae, a New Hope resident, who mustered community support to save the much-loved institution. The curtain rose again in 2012 for a limited season — with planning for full seasons underway.

The theater arts are not only alive in Bucks County, but they are also thriving, with several established theaters, community theaters, and a brand new one.

There's plenty of good theater to be had — and, like art, it is no longer confined only to New Hope, but spread around the county.

The closing ended an era that began when the late showman St. John Terrell created a summer theater in an ancient gristmill in 1939. He stayed with the project only for a year but its future was secured by the likes of Pulitzer Prize-winning dramatist George S. Kaufman and playwright/screenwriter Moss Hart, who did their creative work at their Bucks County farms, escaping the distractions of Broadway. (Kaufman's estate, Barley Sheaf Farm, is now an inn and spa.)

The playhouse had only 450 seats, but it had a huge reputation, drawing its audience from far beyond the county's boundaries. It also served as an incubator for plays, such as "Harvey" and "Barefoot in the Park" that moved on to Broadway. Many actors who crossed

The prelude to what was to have been the final performance at the Bucks County Playhouse in 2010 was as dramatic as anything that appeared on its stage in seven decades. The show, in fact, did not go on.

"A Christmas Carol" was scheduled December 23, but when the actors arrived they found the theatre's doors had been padlocked because the bank was unable to collect on its loan.

It was a bitter, bitter night. The show was sold out and an hour before curtain time ticket-holders began to show up. Some were in furs and diamonds, others in more casual clothes.

"The people were dumbfounded," said Gerry Monigan of New Hope, who witnessed that closing act. "Some were sad, a lot of people just stayed there and milled around.

"There was a couple there from Long Island and Larry Keller, New Hope's mayor, offered to buy them breakfast. Then the actors climbed onto the steps and sang numbers from the show and Christmas carols," Monigan said. "It was very dramatic."

Producer Ralph Miller, who had owned the theatre for thirty-three years but had perpetual financial problems, was unable to raise the $2.2 million he owed and the theatre was closed and put on the auction block.

its stage made their first appearances at New Hope, later joining the ranks of the great.

Just a few were Grace Kelly, Robert Redford, William Shatner, Jack Klugman, Liza Minnelli, John Travolta, and the husband and wife team of George C. Scott and Colleen Dewhurst.

The Bristol Riverside Theatre, about thirty miles south, celebrated its twenty-fifth anniversary in 2011 and draws accolades as a fine regional theater offering a varying program. Funded by the Grundy Foundation established by the town's patriarch, it grew from an old movie theater that had descended to playing pornographic films. It took more than a million dollars to turn it into a state-of-the art three hundred-seat theater.

Operated now by The Repertory Theater of Bucks County, it is known for finding and developing new talent and new plays. The list of celebrities associated with the theater vies with that of the Bucks County Playhouse. They include Katharine Hepburn, Gregory Peck, Kim Hunter, and Keir Dullea, who, incidentally, went to nearby George School.

Bucks County is also home to the Dance Theatre of Pennsylvania. Founded by Marilyn Budzinski, who danced with the Pennsylvania Ballet, the company presents several full-length ballets annually, including "The Nutcracker," a holiday tradition. She is its artistic director, and founded Budzinski Studios of Ballet in Doylestown, the official ballet school of the dance theater, a pre-professional company. Her son, Christopher Budzinski, is a principal dancer with the Pittsburgh Ballet Company.

The Sellersville Theater 1894, in Sellersville in Upper Bucks, is a highly ornate old movie theater handsomely restored. It takes its name from a stable that was built on the site in 1894.

Now, the theater, actually a concert hall that's all Victorian velvet and gold tassels, has a faithful following and draws name acts to the small town that borders Perkasie.

It's been going strong since it was opened in

2002 by William Quigley and his wife, Elayne Brick, restaurateurs who also own The Washington House Restaurant next to the theater. They have made Sellersville a dinner and concert destination.

Grant money turned a disreputable old movie house into the Bristol Riverside Theatre.

Quakertown offers a similar profile. The theater there, once called The Main Street Theatre, is now McCoole's Arts and Events Place and is paired with the historic McCoole's Red Lion Inn. Built in the early 1800s, the building was a livery stable for the inn. It now houses banquet and events rooms on the first floor. The second floor is a stark 193-seat "black box" theater, the type often used for experimental theater.

Smaller community theaters continue to thrive. They include Town and Country Players in Buckingham, a non-profit acting company for sixty years; Langhorne Players, a non-profit, volunteer community theater troupe founded in 1947; the Newtown Theatre Company and the new Monarch Theatre Troupe in nearby Holland.

AMUSEMENTS: THEN AND NOW

The new PARX Casino and Race Track, with its slot machines and table games, is open day and night.

Today, people of all ages flock to Lower Bucks County for fun — but then they've been doing that for more than three hundred years.

Lower Bucks County, where the wealthy once bred their own race horses and gambled among themselves, is now home to PARX, a glittering new casino, where adults can gamble. Or, they can bet on thoroughbreds at the old Philadelphia Park.

Now part of PARX East, which opened last year, the race track was the home of Smarty Jones, the gallant little Pennsylvania-bred stallion who won the Kentucky Derby and the Preakness Stakes in 2004, then came in a heart-breaking second at the Belmont Stakes, the final round of racing's Triple Crown.

Bucks County had a race track as early as 1810, when a physician built the Bath Springs House at the mineral springs of Bath, a tiny and fashionable watering place only a half mile from Bristol, and laid out a race track. Two springs apparently were known to exist there as early as 1700.

By 1720, prominent colonists had begun flocking to Bath to drink and bathe in the yellow waters thought to have curative powers. Bath only faded into history after New York's Saratoga Springs became a magnet for the rich.

For the kids, there's Sesame Place, a gigantic theme park. Folks riding at the top of Sesame Place's Skysplash can see the Philadelphia skyline on a clear day. If they could look into the past as well, they'd see the ghosts of nineteenth century amusement parks.

The proximity of the city certainly played a role in the decision to build Sesame Place near Langhorne, easily reached from several great centers of population.

The theme park, based on the Sesame Street television program and opened in 1980 on three acres, now offers fourteen acres of fun including amazing rides capped off with a Neighborhood Street Party parade with giant floats and Elmo's Cloud Chase, a family ride.

Sesame Place is a distant, sophisticated cousin of the parks and picnic grounds that drew thousands of pleasure seekers more than one hundred years earlier.

By the mid-nineteenth century, the railroads had arrived, bringing expansion, prosperity and tourists to former stage coach centers. By then, Bucks had already become a country haven for Philadelphians, and as travel became speedier and more comfortable, New Yorkers.

The Andalusia Wharf, the first stop in Bucks for northbound steamships and sailing vessels, was a popular destination for day trips from the city. A nearby picnic ground, Chestnut Grove, became a gathering place for schools, societies and private partygoers seeking summertime fun.

By the 1870s, two passenger steamboats were making daily excursions from Philadelphia's Chestnut Street Wharf to Bristol. Amusement parks, some built by railroads to boost ticket sales, began to appear.

One of them, Neshaminy Falls Amusement Park, also called Neshaminy Grove Park, near Oakford, was built in 1876. It once featured prominent lecturers and Sunday afternoon concerts and eventually became a camp meeting.

Penn Valley Amusement Park, claiming it was the largest free amusement park in the world, ran along the Lincoln Highway at Trevose and offered one hundred rides, bathing and picnic grounds. It advertised itself as

being eighteen miles from Philadelphia's City Hall and twelve miles from Trenton, New Jersey.

Another, Forest Park, also called Funk's Park, was established between Pine Run and the Neshaminy Creek near Chalfont in 1885. The 120-acre park had a dining/dancing pavilion, carousel, toboggan ride, bowling alley and dance hall.

Its 75-by-100-foot swimming pool, added in 1928, was supposedly the largest in the country, and as many as 20,000 pleasure-seekers would visit the park on a holiday weekend.

The park closed in the 1960s, and part of it remains the way it was the day it closed. A reminder of that era is a townhouse development on part of its former grounds fittingly called Carousel Pointe. Now, Friends of Forest Park, a new group, is working to preserve the park's history.

Menlo Park in Perkasie was founded in 1892 and its memory has been carefully kept alive in a unique way. Before the town bought the privately owned park in 1955, its 1891 carousel had been replaced by a 1951 carousel. When the park closed in the early 1960s, the town dismantled everything but the carousel.

Now operated and maintained by the Perkasie Historical Society, the carousel is open to the public on certain Sunday afternoons in spring, summer and early fall.

During the early years of amusement parks, the less populated northeastern portion of the county was accessible mostly by horse and carriage. Still, there were special places that drew pleasure seekers. Haycock Mountain, its rocky heights reaching 960 feet, was considered the place to go for picnics.

Remnants of cabins built for camp meetings can still be found in wooded areas near several Upper Bucks villages.

Early nineteenth century pleasure seekers also visited Durham Cave not far from the Delaware in Durham Township. Marked on a 1770 map, the cavern was composed of three large rooms on separate levels. A Lenni Lenape village was situated near the entrance. Crystal formations gave the cavern, "a startlingly beautiful appearance," according to one visitor.

By 1850, though, tourists, breaking off pieces of crystal and rock had already taken their toll at the site and stone at the cave had been broken up commercially and sold. All that remains of the cavern today is the opening, which is on private property. It probably was the earliest cave known to pioneers.

The Delaware Division of the Pennsylvania Canal which by then had snaked its way along the River Road between Bristol and Easton was a constant draw for sightseers, as it is today, and a place called Jugtown in Tinicum Township was a popular resort. The riverbank there was dotted with inns and summer boarding houses attracting city guests.

1: A jockey calms his mount in the paddock before an afternoon race at the track.

2: The Sesame Place theme park offers fourteen acres of fun.

3: Perkasie took over when an amusement park closed. Now, it offers rides on a community carousel on some Sunday afternoons.

TO BROWSE, TO SHOP

The Den, a store for men, is just one of the seventy shops at Peddler's Village.

Peddler's Village is the vision-turned-reality of a man whose ancestors operated a Lahaska tavern known as Jamison's.

Marking its fiftieth anniversary in 2012, the shopping/dining village is one of three landmark shopping centers that were once just small roadside markets. (In addition, two major malls, Oxford Valley and Neshaminy, provide good shopping, as do any number of boutiques and stores.)

That early tavern, a stop for stagecoach passengers traveling between Philadelphia and New York, was opened by Henry Jamison in 1763 in a crossroads village then called Centreville.

After two centuries had passed, one of his descendants, the late Earl Hart Jamison, founded Peddler's Village a mile away from the original tavern on the remains of an old chicken hatchery. He built fourteen shops and the Cock 'n Bull Restaurant on the six-acre property.

Today, an estimated 1.7 million people a year stroll the brick paths winding their way through the colorful gardens and shops that comprise this romantic vision of shopping in Colonial America.

The village, which now covers forty-two acres, houses seventy specialty shops, six restaurants, the Golden Plough Inn, and Giggleberry Fair, a family entertainment center. Outdoor festivals are frequent and weddings on the green are popular. Just across Old York Road is Penn's Purchase Factory Outlet, a collection of forty shops.

A sign outside the original Jamison's Tavern identifies it as the General Greene Inn, but it has been an antique/junk shop for as long as most natives can remember.

Headquarters for General Nathanael Greene in 1777, it also was the place the county's Revolutionary recruits first mustered. At one time the building was called Bogart's Tavern.

In 1955, before his village enterprise took root, Jamison had operated a roadside produce market which he turned into Bountiful Acres, a garden center and nursery. Now owned by another family, it remains a Buckingham landmark.

Rice's Sale & Country Market in nearby Solebury was something that "just happened" in 1860 when A. L. Rice, a farmer who owned the land where the market now stands decided to auction his farm produce. He conducted sporadic sales and soon his neighbors joined the enterprise, auctioning their own animals and produce.

Eventually, livestock auctions were staged every Tuesday. In the 1950s an outdoor flea market was started by owners Bobby and Barbara Blanche. The flea market is open every Tuesday all year long from 7 a.m. until 1 p.m. and on Saturdays from March to December.

The thirty-acre market is a magnet for Bucks County matrons who for years have regularly risen before dawn, and rain or shine, raced off to Rice's hoping to get there "before the good stuff is gone."

What brings them back again and again is that oft repeated phrase, "You never know what you'll find." The products and vendors can and do shift with the wind, but many of the same open-air merchants are always there enthusiastically selling their wares. Their chatter, more global than local these days, encompasses the accents of many nations, and is part of the charm.

What is now the Quakertown Farmers Market also had unplanned beginnings. In 1932, a farmer named Stanley Rotenberg decided to sell farm equipment, feed and crafts at his farm near Quakertown. Open only on Saturdays, it was the only market for miles around and for years it really had no name. It was simply called The Sale.

In the 1940s, the Woldow family bought it and it is now operated by Richard Woldow, grandson of the patriarch Mark Woldow, who named it the Quakertown Farmers Market.

Local businesses started to rent space and sell their goods in the market. At one point produce was sold in a row of open stands and livestock auctions were a popular draw until 1990. Much of the market was under roof, and 50,000 to 60,000 people would pass through on a weekend.

John R. Chism, who's managed the market for sixteen years and is a past president of the National Flea Market Association, says, "This was the area's first true department store, a collection of independent vendors selling their wares. We were actually an incubator for new businesses, some now in their fifth generation."

The market, open Fridays through Sundays, has a huge indoor/outdoor flea market and there are a couple delicatessens and a bakery. Bargain-hunters can have a rollicking good time dropping only a few dollars or a lot, buying anything from fresh peaches and Vidalia onions to geodes and fossils. Farm fresh produce and meats continue to draw crowds as do special events scheduled throughout the year.

1: Weddings often take place at the village with guests
mingling in the Victorian gazebo.

2: A sparkling carousel is a highlight at Giggleberry Fair,
the children's area at Peddler's Village.

3: Ki Huyon Kim stacks cucumbers at his produce stand at
Quakertown Farmers Market.

4: Shoppers often lose themselves amidst the variety of
handbags at Rice's Sale & Country Market.

Langhorne's old town hall goes back to the days when fire engines were smaller. These doors are only about seven feet wide.

anghorne and Newtown, like Doylestown, are islands of history caught between waves of successive housing developments, and have fought hard to retain their individual identities.

Both are built around districts on the National Register of Historic Places and the old buildings meld happily with all the assets of today's prosperous and busy communities.

Towns like these don't just stay the way they were; they are preserved by residents who care about the past enough to fight off those who would either knock down or pave over to make something new. Both the Historic Langhorne Association and Newtown Historic Association have contributed to that effort to blend old and new successfully.

Ironically, both towns were originally little real estate developments and both are old Quaker communities settled in the late seventeenth century. Newtown itself was laid out by Penn's surveyor, Thomas Holme, in 1684; Penn himself is said to have named it.

In 1691, the Middletown Friends Meeting in Langhorne established the first library with twenty-three religious books; twenty-seven years later it had accumulated about three hundred.

Today, a later library, a red-brick Victorian dedicated in 1889, is home to the Historic Langhorne Association, as well as a research library and museum. The community is also served by the Langhorne Branch of Bucks County Public Library.

In the 1720s Samuel Richardson opened a general store, and a community called Four Lanes End grew up around it at the crossroads of two Indian paths, one that would become Durham Road, the other the Old Lincoln Highway.

The town's name was later changed to Attleboro, and to its present name in 1876 to honor Jeremiah Langhorne, a chief Justice of the Pennsylvania Supreme Court. The judge lived in high style in the town, but was kind to his slaves and eventually set them free.

Both towns also played roles in the American Revolution. Newtown was a supply depot for Washington's

troops during his campaigns in New Jersey. He set up headquarters in a stone house on Sycamore Street shortly before and after the famous river crossing in 1776.

Hessian troops captured in the Battle of Trenton were also held at the Old Presbyterian Church before they were marched to Philadelphia for a prisoner exchange. Twenty-two Revolutionary soldiers are buried in the church graveyard. Today the old church, built in 1769, is used only for summer services.

Dr. William Shippen Sr., Washington's surgeon-general, established a hospital for troops who were ill or injured after the Battle of Trenton at four buildings, including the Middleton Friends Meeting and School, in what is now Langhorne.

Word of the burial of as many as 166 Revolutionary soldiers in the center of town had passed down through generations. With the help of Temple University's Department of Anthropology, that sad legend was revealed to be true. The property is now preserved as a small park and marked with a granite monument, a flagpole, a memorial bench, and flowers.

Both Langhorne and Newtown share the bragging rights for artist Edward Hicks. Born in Langhorne and reared in Newtown Township, the Quaker minister and folk artist owned a shop in Newtown where he painted signs and coaches and a series of Peaceable Kingdom paintings that have made him world-famous. He lived in Newtown until his death in 1849, when his burial service at the Friends Meeting graveyard reportedly drew 5,000 mourners.

Newtown Borough and Township share the distinction of having recently been named a Preserve

America community by the White House. Along with Durham Township, they are the only such communities in Bucks County and among just eight hundred throughout the country.

1: Owned by the Historic Langhorne Association, this red brick Victorian is now home to a research library and museum.

2: Interesting little shops line Newtown's Main Street.

3: Edward Hicks, painter of the prized Peaceable Kingdom primitives, lived in this house on Newtown's Penn Street from 1821 to 1849.

A FINE CLIMATE FOR GRAPES

Sand Castle Winery was built to resemble a castle in Czechoslovakia.

1: In the spring, wisteria covers the old walls of Nicholas Biddle's graperies.

2: The vineyards at Sand Castle Winery in Tinicum Township offer a seventeen-mile view of rolling hills.

Grape vines are a part of Bucks County's official seal, but there were no commercial wineries in the county before the middle of the nineteenth century. Now there are about twenty, and the tasting, pairings and purchase of the fruit of the vine are an important part of the county's economy.

Interestingly enough, two Czechoslovakian brothers who moved to Bucks County in 1969 actually succeeded at a task that stopped William Penn and his servants in their tracks three hundred years earlier.

Like Penn, the Maxian brothers, Joseph and Paul, imported grape vines from Europe, but they also spent decades preparing the soil before they dared to plant vines. The brothers have established a successful vineyard in Tinicum Township high above the Delaware River.

Penn had not been so lucky. Hoping to establish a vineyard at Pennsbury Manor, he imported grapevines from Europe and had them planted at the manor but the enterprise was not a successful one.

In the 1830s, another gentleman farmer, Nicholas Biddle, tried to grow grapes at Andalusia, his estate in Bensalem Township. He wanted the grapes, not for wine, but for his own table and for sale in Philadelphia. The first rounds of grapes fell victim to brutal winters and Biddle eventually realized he had to protect the grapes from the weather. So, he built an enormous glass-paned hothouse heated with steam made from water drawn from the Delaware.

He called it "the grapery" and it reportedly produced grapes in profusion, so many that he sold them at Philadelphia markets and gave some to the poor. A portion of the grapery wall still stands and in April it is draped in wisteria, a vision the Andalusia staff, and visitors as well, look forward to every year.

The Maxians named their venture Sand Castle Winery and built a castle modeled after one in their native Bratislava in Czechoslovakia.

It is just one of the wineries linked together in the Bucks County Wine Trail. Members believe Bucks County is becoming one of the premier wine-producing areas in the country. At last count, about half of the wineries in the county are part of the trail.

The Wine Trail is a destination for tourists but it is also popular with the locals who stage weddings, private parties and corporate events in romantic vineyard surroundings. The member wineries take part in seasonal self-driving tours, promising "World class wines. Minutes Apart," and most offer full schedules of tastings, classes, wine and cheese pairings and concerts ranging from jazz to chamber music.

At Sand Castle, situated on a hilltop, the white castle towers over the 72-acre European-style winery and offers a seventeen-mile view of the hills and woods in Pennsylvania and across the river in New Jersey.

Sand Castle is one of the few wineries on the East Coast growing only European vines, and it relies entirely on its own harvest with the entire process taking place at the estate. "This is a special place," Maxian says. "It has the sunshine of Italy, the winters of northern Germany and open rocky soils."

In fact, in 1984, an entire 24-mile stretch along the river from just north of Kintnersville reaching south to Bowman's Hill near Washington Crossing was designated by the federal government as the Central Delaware Valley Viticulture District. Covering 96,000 acres, the grape-growing area crosses the river and extends into Hunterdon County in New Jersey.

RISING FROM
THE ASHES

A Perkasie street has nineteenth century charm, especially
during the Christmas season.

Antiques look right at home in an old shop in town.

The office of Grim, Biehn & Thatcher, the second oldest and largest law firm in Upper Bucks County, is in Perkasie.

The town of Perkasie, like the legendary phoenix, has risen from its own ashes — twice. And both times the citizens of Perkasie have united — not only to repair the damage but also to look to the future.

Perkasie is an old town, but a big part of it is new. Occupied by the British in the winter of 1777-1778, it rose to prominence as a railroad town in the mid-1800s and was a center for cigar and baseball factories. By the mid 1900s, it prided itself as an All-American typical small town.

In 1988, the afternoon of June 26 was warm and sunny, but increasingly high winds shook the trees and shoved sailboats off course in nearby lakes.

Smoke began to curl up and spread its blinding barrier over Seventh and Market streets in the old town. Then came flames, a frenzied fire call, the shrieking sirens — and the boys who started it all were in big trouble.

About three hundred firefighters from about fifty companies from Bucks and surrounding counties, responded to the desperate fire call. Despite all the firefighters with their modern equipment and technology could do, fire roared like an angry beast though the heart of Perkasie, destroying about fifteen percent of the town. When the smoke cleared, a number of historic buildings had been lost and part of the town's past had been wiped out.

Just two years short of a century earlier, a disastrous fire had struck the center of town, destroying twelve buildings. On June 8, 1890, residents fought the blaze using their own buckets and ladders but could do little to stop its spread. The fire had started at a livery stable at Seventh and Chestnut streets.

Within a month of that first monster fire, a committee had gathered to organize a fire company and by September the 32-member Hope Fire Company was ready for action.

Immediately after what has been called the Great Fire of Perkasie in 1988, a task force of borough officials, businessmen and home owners put together a five-year town improvement plan.

The ideas they turned into action brought new life to the area affected by the massive fire. The shade trees they planted have matured. The ugly utility wires that steal from the beauty of other old towns in the county disappeared underground. Handsome new but old-fashioned streetlights brighten the Town Square at night and benches line the new sidewalks.

The town looks better than ever. It has an open, airy and welcoming feel to it and it's the perfect place for the town's community Christmas tree.

The oldest community Christmas tree in the country is said to be the one that lights up the town square in Perkasie Borough every year.

It is believed the tradition, which includes a lighting ceremony the first Saturday in December, was started in 1909, after the owner of the town newspaper, now known at *The Perkasie News Herald*, had visited a neighbor to see his tree and conceived the idea of lighting an outdoor tree for the whole community to enjoy.

Newspaper reporters seeking to authenticate the claim discovered a 1914 newspaper article that referred to the tradition's fifth year, setting its establishment in 1909.

Perkasie was the first town in the country to decorate a community Christmas tree.

That means the Perkasie Christmas tree was lighted three years before a community tree in Madison Square Park in New York City in 1912, and Colonial Williamsburg in 1915.

Now the Perkasie Olde Towne Association erects and decorates a thirty-foot-tall blue spruce and invites the community to attend its lighting ceremony.

The fact that Perkasie is the first community to have a tree actually comes as no surprise. Although the town was built on land that was Perkasie Manor, one of William Penn's estates, many of its settlers had come from Germany where Christmas trees originated.

Sellersville, tucked next to Perkasie and to its west, really didn't come to life as a community until the North Pennsylvania Railroad arrived in the 1860s. Soon, a thriving textile industry was established and brought workers to the area. Industry is long gone and Sellersville people have kept their homes but have found jobs elsewhere. It's now a bedroom community caught between housing developments.

WHITEWATER
AND MORE

Kayakers paddle through the whitewater in Tohickon Creek.

The Delaware River and its tributaries offer lots of fun both on the water and in the water. The lakes scattered throughout the county also attract those interested in water sports.

For the truly adventurous whitewater kayaking on the Tohickon Creek is great. Twice a year, water is released from the dam at Lake Nockamixon, creating a whitewater paradise as it races toward the river.

From afar, the colorful kayakers look like rubber duckies bobbing through the swirling whitewater as they approach the antique bridge over the Tohickon Creek at Point Pleasant.

A helmeted man in a wetsuit gives a thumbs-up as he pulls his kayak from the water after a four-mile downstream ride from Ralph Stover State Park. He has chosen to end his adventure here instead of continuing on to the Delaware River as others do.

In March and November when conditions are right, water is released from the dam at Lake Nockamixon into the creek. Enthusiasts wait at Stover Park to meet the whitewater. They don wetsuits and flotation devices, grab their paddles, and launch their watercraft for a swift and splash-filled ride past eddies and over rock ledges, and through a natural landscape as dramatic as it is beautiful as the water tumbles and crashes toward the river.

The rush of water from the 1,400-acre lake is considered technical whitewater with Class 3 and 4 rapids and it requires great skill to negotiate. The creek, with its drop-offs and obstructions can be very dangerous, but officials say about 1,500 boaters enjoy the whitewater during each release. They come from all over the mid-Atlantic region to confront the watery challenge.

More frequently, local kayakers can be seen ripping through the rocks and dropping off the ledges. These unscheduled excursions usually follow heavy rains when the water is still high and roaring through the valley.

Kayakers enjoy less intensive paddling on the Delaware River and on portions of the Delaware Canal that roughly follows the course of the river south from the City of Easton, where it meets the Lehigh Canal, to Bristol.

In fact, the river north of the Falls is a great watery playground for all kinds of water sports and in the warm weather is abuzz with boaters and jet skiers.

Bucks County River Country, founded by Thomas McBrien more than forty years ago, is headquartered in Point Pleasant and rents kayaks, canoes and rafts and organizes tubing trips. Tubers are transported upriver by the busload and float down the river, ending at a sandy beach where they can relax at a riverside café. Tubers can opt for three- or four-hour river trips. Snuggle tubes allow a parent and small child to travel together.

When the moon is full, nighttime boating, complete with glow-in-the dark bracelets and guides, is a great way to experience the wonders of the river.

A cruise aboard the *River Otter* is a nice recreational option for those who prefer more passive recreation and regard elbow-bending as a sport. The Bucks County Riverboat and Trolley Companies, based at Keller's Landing in Upper Black Eddy, offers sunset cocktail cruises. The pontoon boat with its Riverboat Pub cruises the river near Upper Black Eddy, a particularly scenic and unspoiled area, for about an hour and a half before sunset on weekends. It is also available for parties and weddings, according to Captain Dee Keller. The trolley delivers passengers to the pontoon boat and collects corporate and party groups.

But the pontoon boat is not just for fun. In a student program, The Delaware River Experience, children collect samples of aquatic life aboard the River Otter and return to a living science laboratory/classroom at the landing to learn about ecology and environmental concerns.

1: Whitewater enthusiasts gather their colorful gear at the side of the creek.

2: Sailboats glide through the waters of Lake Nockamixon in Nockamixon State Park.

3: This windsurfer found conditions perfect at Lake Galena in Peace Valley County Park.

4: Boats dock at the marina at Nockamixon State Park.

A SENSE OF READINESS

A late eighteenth century building being restored on Springtown's Main Street will be a museum.

One of Springfield Township's main centers of population is Springtown, which is larger than a village and smaller than a town, and lies snug against the foot of Springtown Hill.

There, Route 212, lined with eighteenth century stone houses, doubles as Main Street. The old stone Springtown Inn stands guard over a mix of Victorian styles. The street has remained mostly untouched in the past forty years, but now change is arriving.

An eighteenth century building in town is being privately restored by the Upper Bucks Agricultural Collective, a group headed by John Heinz IV, who lives in Tinicum, and plans to open a museum and retail shops when work is completed, bringing new life to a long shuttered, complex of buildings on Main Street.

The more than 2,000-square-foot museum will house Heinz's collection of old cooking utensils and artifacts.

"We think it was once a house and could have been built as early as 1790 but there's no paperwork to support that," said Bradley Sullivan of Sullivan Building & Design Group, the company restoring the property.

A few surprises cropped up as workers stripped the building. Early renovations had covered original features, such as doorways, or blocked a fireplace or stairway. One fireplace wasn't really where workers thought it was, but they found it, and that, too, has been restored.

Sullivan said the restoration will take the structure back to its original state. That means no electricity and no plumbing. Workers even made some of the tools they needed; lost or damaged parts no longer available also had to be made by hand.

a processing shanty for meat and sausage. Farmers also made apple butter and cider there and did the laundry, according to a study completed by Bucks County Community College. It also showed evidence of being an early residence.

1: The restoration shows the simple elegance of an Early American spiral staircase.

2: The little log kitchen at this Springfield Township farm once served as a residence.

Toward the other end of town, passersby see only the top story of one charming little house built way below road level. It apparently was a cabin at the foot of the hill and when the owners needed more space, they just built on top of the first cabin and again on top of the second level.

In direct contrast to the old, an all-green development of energy-efficient homes is situated just outside town.

An interesting farm near Springtown is Meadow Brook Farms owned by Nevada Mease who sells grass-fed beef. The older section of the farmhouse was built in 1810, the newer in 1854, and the foundation dates from the 1700s. It's part of a large farming complex on Slifer Valley Road.

Standing close to Cooks Creek on the farm is the Slifer log kitchen. Built in the early nineteenth century, it measures about twelve by twenty feet, and served as

For generations, art, too, has sprung from the soil of Springfield Township. The 150-acre Kirkland Farm was once owned by playwright, Jack Kirkland, who adapted Erskine Caldwell's *Tobacco Road* for Broadway.

It was the first home of his daughter, the celebrated dancer Gelsey Kirkland, who partnered with Mikhail Baryshnikov in the American Ballet Theatre.

That artistic tradition continues today with Silo/Kirkland Farm, a non-profit dance residency program that encourages the creation and development of new work.

The farm, owned by Robin Staff, artistic director of Dancenow [NYC], and her husband, Marty, offers urban dancers free rehearsal space and low-cost housing for a few days or weeks at a time.

Carol C. Dorey, who owns The Hollow, a country estate that once covered more than five hundred acres in Springfield and Durham townships, has a collection of old deeds and maps.

Several of the oldest deeds for The Hollow bear clay seals made of soil from the property.

After the original deeds were written, the new owner received a small ball of soil from the property. Deed and dirt were then shipped to England where the soil would be turned into a clay tablet to be imprinted with an official seal, attached to the document with a silk ribbon or cord, and returned to the landowner.

Dorey's oldest deed dates from 1740 and bears the signatures of Richard and Thomas Penn, sons of William Penn.

Another acknowledges the power of both the reigning English king and God. It reads "…in the 15th year of our sovereign lord George III by the grace of God, king over Great Britain, and in the year of our lord 1775…."

Just north of Springtown, the county's more serious hills begin. The tallest, Flint Hill, rising from both Springfield Township and neighboring Lehigh County, reaches a height of 975 feet with wondrous views of both Springfield and the Lehigh Valley. A drive along Route 212,

which cuts across the county's northern edge, offers a continuous panoramic view of the Durham Hills, foothills of the Appalachian Mountains.

Springfield's scenery in general is impressive with rugged hills and deep valleys running along Cooks Creek and still relatively undisturbed by civilization. Settled mostly by Germans, it became a township in 1743.

1: The 110-foot-long Knecht's Bridge, built of hemlock in 1873, crosses Cook's Creek in Slifer Valley.

2: Cook's Creek winds its way through Springfield and Durham townships.

TOWNS THAT LOOK NORTH

The Liberty Bell was hidden overnight behind Quakertown's Liberty Hall when patriots took it to Allentown to hide it from the British.

Quakertown and Riegelsville, the two "big" towns in the northern reaches of the county, could not be more different. Both, though, were transportation centers and both look north toward the Lehigh Valley.

The railroad brought commerce to Quakertown in the 1850s, but it was the Delaware Division of the Pennsylvania Canal that jolted Riegelsville into action two decades earlier.

Commerce is centered around Quakertown's downtown, but the town also is largely a bedroom community, with its residents working elsewhere. With a downtown revival underway, it grows more attractive every year. It is surrounded by new housing developments and an even newer stretch of shopping centers on Route 309, still a main road from Philadelphia to Bethlehem and Allentown.

Quakertown, closer to the City of Bethlehem than it is to the county seat in Doylestown, was carved out of a true wilderness, and was little more than a few stone buildings when the American Revolution brought its big excitement to town.

That happened in September 1777, when patriots driving farm wagons carried the Liberty Bell from Philadelphia to a hiding place in Allentown to the north so the British would not capture it and melt it for cannon shot.

The journey was a long one and the group stopped, hid the bell behind the home of Evan Foulke, now Liberty Hall, on Quakertown's Broad Street, and stayed overnight at McCoole's Tavern on the corner.

The 262-year old stone building has seen its ups and downs, but it's established now as McCoole's at the Historic

121

Red Lion Inn, a restaurant and bar. The German-born tax protesters who plotted the Fries Rebellion there in 1799 would certainly recognize it. They feared the taxes meant a return to British rule, rebelled, were arrested and mercifully saved from hanging by none other than John Adams.

After the arrival of the Quakers, German immigrants had turned the surrounding woods into farmland and the towns still honors its German heritage.

The town came into its own only when the Reading Railroad arrived in the mid-nineteenth century. The Civil War brought new business in a big way and farmland started to give way to manufacturing sites. The granite passenger station with a chestnut-paneled interior was not built until 1902. It has been restored as a local landmark along the tracks that run through town.

Riegelsville has always had its head turned toward the City of Easton, just nine miles to the north in Northampton County.

It was founded on the Delaware River toward the end of the eighteenth century and developed later as a tight little company town with the requisite showcase mansion of the founding family. Its first business was a ferry established in 1774. When Benjamin Riegel, a farmer, bought the property in 1806, taking over the ferry and erecting buildings, he gave the town his name.

In 1832, construction of the Delaware Canal opened the town to commerce and the Riegel dynasty began its reign. The Riegels built a bridge across the Delaware in 1838 to replace the ferry. That covered wooden bridge was swept away by a flood in 1903 and replaced with a steel wire bridge the following year.

In 2004, the townspeople marked the bridge's centennial with a parade of antique cars and a community party. The suspension bridge, constructed by John A. Roebling & Sons Co., builder of the Brooklyn Bridge, is unique. Bridge people believe it may be one of a kind. Now on the National Register of Historic Places, it still carries traffic and remains a source of community pride.

John Leidy Riegel of the family's fifth generation created the family's fortunes with his paper mills, providing jobs for generations of workers on both sides of the river and established a coed academy and a library in 1886.

Benjamin Franklin Fackenthal Jr., who married a Riegel daughter, built his imposing home, Glacialdrift, on Mansion Row on a ridge high above sea level in 1895. The Fackenthals were friends of Henry Ford and Thomas Edison. Frequent visitors to the mansion which now is Villa Richard, a restaurant and bed-and-breakfast inn, were Theodore Roosevelt and Henry Cabot Lodge Sr.

After that period Riegelsville lost much of its luster as the mills closed and most of the Riegels moved away. The lower part of town has always been plagued by floods; most recently three in only eighteen months in 2004-2006.

As the town aged, newcomers seeking small town ambiance arrived, breathing new life into the community as well as a welcome friendliness and a new creative energy.

Prize-winning children's book illustrator Ponder Goembel, lives in Riegelsville in a 150-year-old home. Her latest book is *Animal Fair*, published by Marshall-Cavendish.

Bil Mitchell, a luthier, works in a tiny shop on Durham Road in the center of town.

1: Quakertown's train station, a 110-year-old landmark, has been restored.

2: The Riegelsville Inn, nestled between canal and river, has been a popular dining spot since the town's founder built it in 1838.

3: The one-of-a-kind Roebling suspension bridge at Riegelsville marked its 100th anniversary in 2004.

"AFTER DARKNESS... LIGHT"

The gateway opens onto the Memorial Path that leads to the fountains.

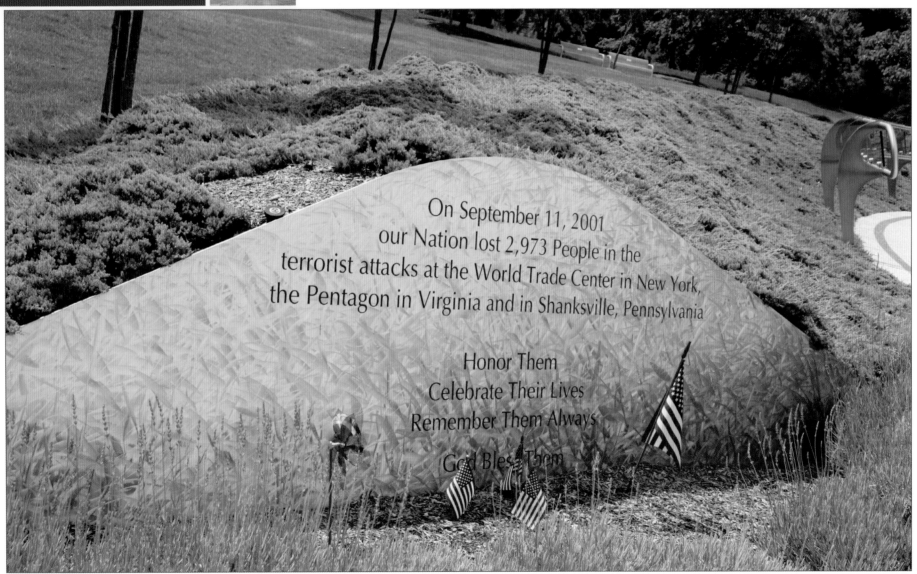

On September 11, 2001 our Nation lost 2,973 People in the terrorist attacks at the World Trade Center in New York, the Pentagon in Virginia and in Shanksville, Pennsylvania

Honor Them
Celebrate Their Lives
Remember Them Always

God Bless Them

124

1: The twin fountains at the Garden of Reflection honor the victims of the September 11, 2001, terrorist attacks.

2: Flags mark the graves of unknown Revolutionary soldiers buried by the river at Washington Crossing Historic Park.

t is a great triangle of remembrance — the Garden of Reflection, the new Veterans National Cemetery at Washington Crossing and the solemn line of tombstones marking the graves of Revolutionary soldiers at Washington Crossing Park — all within a few miles of each other.

It's also a comfort to know that symbolism matters to those who make big decisions about the placement of such monuments.

In a county as old as Bucks, memorials honoring lost heroes abound. There's a public monument in practically every small community; but none is so touching, so splendid as the Garden of Reflection, Pennsylvania's official memorial to the victims of September 11, 2001.

The twin fountains piercing the sky from empty squares that signify the footprints of the twin towers produce instant tears — perhaps because the impact of the horrendous attacks is still so raw. Eighteen Bucks Countians were among the victims — on the hijacked airplanes and in the World Trade Center. These were our people, bristling with life, sharing our dreams and troubles, and they are gone too soon.

In Lower Makefield Township, the Garden of Reflection is a stunning tribute to the 2,973 people killed in the terrorist attacks in New York City and the Pentagon and to those brave men who gave their lives to bring down a fourth hijacked plane in western Pennsylvania.

Designed by architect Liuba Lashchyk of nearby Yardley, the memorial garden overflows with symbolism. The entrance is a flag circle leading to a tear-shaped court that holds broken steel beams from the World Trade Center.

At Remembrance Walk, the names of all the victims are etched on glass panels along the walk with keystone symbols marking the names of Pennsylvania victims.

The twin fountains dominate the Memorial Core of the garden with a Circle of Reflection bearing panels

etched with the names of Bucks County victims. Nine red maple trees honor the Lower Makefield victims. On the Spiral Walk maples pay tribute to the Bucks County victims and forty-two small luminaries represent the Pennsylvania children who lost parents in the attacks.

The garden is a living memorial carrying the message of "After Darkness…Light" in an attempt to provide a healing peace to those who mourn.

Dedicated in 2006, the memorial is the work of Ellen Saracini, Grace Godshalk, Bill Kelly, Tara Bane, Clara Chirchirillo, and Fiona Havlish, all of whom lost loved ones in the attack and organized and served on The Garden of Reflection Family Committee.

When the federal Department of Veterans Affairs settled on a Bucks County site for its national cemetery, it was called "a setting worthy of their service." Situated on 205 acres of prime real estate in Upper Makefield Township, it, like the Garden of Reflection, is only a few miles from the Revolutionary soldiers' graves at Washington Crossing Historic Park.

The new veterans cemetery has been open only since January 2010 and already the precise lines of white marble markers are beginning to look as though they stretch into eternity. Burials were taking place daily and mourners were visiting graves even before the imposing entrance gates were constructed.

At the Revolutionary Soldiers graves in the nearby park, the tombstones are also white. There American flags fly over a single line of symbolic white tombstones memorializing the remains of twenty-two men in sight of the river the troops crossed to win the Battle of Trenton.

These men were not killed in battle, but died from unhealed wounds, from disease, poor nutrition, exposure, and exhaustion. Soldiers were treated at temporary hospitals in homes along the way; many survived, but the men honored here did not.

Their names remain unknown, with the exception of one. Captain-Lieutenant James Moore of Lamb's Company, New York Artillery, died on Christmas Day 1776 of camp fever at the Thompson-Neely House, which had been turned into a hospital even before the Battle of Trenton.

During work at the park and especially when the Delaware Canal that passes through it was dug in the 1830s, partial remains of soldiers were often found. The present twenty-two graves are only representations of the forty to sixty unknown soldiers believed buried on park grounds.

The Soldier's Graves were officially dedicated in 1964. The base of the flagpole contains native stone from each of the thirteen original colonies.

Visitors mourn their dead at the new Washington Crossing Veterans Cemetery.

BIBLIOGRAPHY

Battle, J. H. *History of Bucks County, Pennsylvania*. Chicago, Illinois: A. Warner & Co., 1887.

Book Committee, Historical Society of Bensalem. *Bensalem III: The Journey Continues*. Mercerville, New Jersey: Van Sant Publishing, 2008.

Brandt, Francis Burke. *The Majestic Delaware: The Nation's Foremost Historic River*. Union City, New Jersey: Wm. H. Wise & Co., Inc., 1981.

Bush, George S., Editor. *The Genius Belt*. Doylestown, Pennsylvania: James A. Michener Art Museum in association with The Pennsylvania State University Press, 1996.

Carey, E. L., and Hunt A. *Philadelphia in 1830-31, or a Brief Account of the Various Institutions and Public Objects in this Metropolis*. Philadelphia, Pennsylvania: James Kay Jun. & Co., 1830.

Davis, W.W.H. *History of Bucks County, Pennsylvania from the Discovery of the Delaware to the Present Time*. Doylestown, Pennsylvania: Democrat Book and Job Office Printers, 1876; and Revised Edition, New York, Chicago, Lewis Publishing Company, 1905.

Donehoo, George P. *Pennsylvania: A History, Volume II*. New York, Chicago, Lewis Historical Publishing Company Inc., 1926.

Fulp, Marjorie Goldthorp, and Varkony, Pamela Feist. *Our Lost Tohickon Valley*. Haycock Township, Pennsylvania: Haycock Historical Society, 2010.

Green, Doron. *A History of the Old Homes on Radcliffe Street*. Bristol Pennsylvania: published privately, 1938.

Kraft, Herbert C. *The Lenape-Delaware Indian Heritage, 10,000 B.C. to A.D. 2000*. Stanhope, New Jersey: Lenape Lifeways Inc., Copyright 2001.

Laubach, Charles. Selections from "A Collection of Papers Read Before the Bucks County Historical Society, Volumes II and III." Easton, Pennsylvania: Press of the Chemical Publishing Company, 1909.

Lebegern, George F. Jr. *Episodes in Bucks County History*. Printed in the United States of America: Bucks County Historical-Tourist Commission, 1975.

Lefferts, Walter. *The Settlement and Growth of Pennsylvania*. Philadelphia, Pennsylvania: Franklin Publishing and Supply Company, 1922.

MacReynolds, George. *Place Names in Bucks County, Pennsylvania*. Doylestown, Pennsylvania: The Bucks County Historical Society, 1955.

McNealy, Terry A. *Bucks County: An Illustrated History*. Doylestown, Pennsylvania: Bucks County Historical Society, 2001.

Patton, Alfreda. *Frankenfield Kin & Family Data*. York, Pennsylvania: published privately, 1987.

Penn, William. *William Penn's Own Account of the Lenni Lenape or Delaware Indians*. Revised Edition: Albert Cook Myers, Editor. Somerset, New Jersey: The Middle Atlantic Press, 1970.

Richie, Margaret Bye, Milner, John D., and Huber, Gregory D. *Stone House: Traditional Homes of Pennsylvania's Bucks County and Brandywine Valley*. New York, New York: Rizzoli International Publications, 2005.

Rivinus, Willis M. *Early Taverns of Bucks County*. New Hope, Pennsylvania: published privately, 1965.
   William Penn and the Lenape Indians. New Hope, Pennsylvania: published privately, 1995.

Secor, Robert, General Editor. *Pennsylvania 1776*. University Park and London: The Pennsylvania State University Press, 1975.

Shoemaker, Ann G. "The Early History of the Delaware Valley Indians: The Red Man in Bucks County," a typewritten research paper containing information gathered between 1919 and 1944, filed at the Spruance Library of the Bucks County Historical Society, Doylestown, Pennsylvania.

Vieira, M. Laffitte. "Historic Club: The State in Schuylkill," *West Philadelphia Illustrated*, Philadelphia, Pennsylvania: Anvil Printing Company, 1903, Copyright 1903 by Charles H. Clarke.

Warburton, Jessie Mabel. *The Margerum Family of Bucks County, Pennsylvania*. Morrisville, Pennsylvania: published privately, 1987.

Weslager, C. A. *The Delaware Indians: A History*. New Brunswick, New Jersey: Rutgers University Press, 1972.

Looking for even more information?

Nearly every place mentioned in this book has a website listing directions, contacts, and providing information about hours and admission, and www.buckscounty.org lists all municipalities.

Here are a few others:

www.visitbuckscounty.com

www.hsp.org

www.explorepahistory.com

www.antislaverystudies.org

http://jerseyman-historynowandthen.blogspot.com

INDEX